Multicultural and Diversity Education

•◆ A REFERENCE HANDBOOK

Other Titles in
ABC-CLIO's
CONTEMPORARY EDUCATION ISSUES
Series

African American Education, Cynthia L. Jackson
The Assessment Debate, Valerie J. Janesick
Bilingual Education, Rosa Castro Feinberg
Charter Schools, Danny Weil
Educational Leadership, Pat Williams-Boyd
Migrant Education, Judith A. Gouwens
Sex, Youth, and Sex Education, David Campos
Special Education, Arlene Sacks
Student Rights, Patricia H. Hinchey
Teacher Training, David B. Pushkin

FORTHCOMING

Alternative Schools, Brenda J. Conley
Educational Reform, Raymond A. Horn, Jr.
Literacy and Learning, Brett Elizabeth Blake and Robert W. Blake
School Vouchers and Privatization, Danny Weil

Multicultural and Diversity Education

● A REFERENCE HANDBOOK

Peter Appelbaum

A B C ● C L I O

Santa Barbara, California • Denver, Colorado • Oxford, England

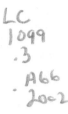
Library of Congress Cataloging-in-Publication Data

Appelbaum, Peter Michael.
  Multicultural and diversity education : a reference handbook / Peter Appelbaum.
       p. cm.— (Contemporary education issues)
Includes bibliographical references (p.) and index.
  ISBN 1-57607-264-9 (alk. paper) ISBN 1-57607-747-0 (e-book)
   1. Multicultural education — United States — Handbooks, manuals, etc.
   2. Educational equalization — United States — Handbooks, manuals, etc.
I. Title. II. Series.
  LC1099.3 .A66 2002
  370.117—dc21   2002011678

This book is also available on the World Wide Web as an e-book.
Visit www.abc-clio.com for details.

07 06 05 04 03 02   10 9 8 7 6 5 4 3 2 1

ABC-CLIO, Inc.
130 Cremona Drive, P.O. Box 1911
Santa Barbara, California 93116-1911

This book is printed on acid-free paper ∞.
Manufactured in the United States of America

For Noah, Sophia, and Terra,
who get to keep the hope in struggle

☛ Contents

❧ Series Editor's Preface

The Contemporary Education Issues series is dedicated to providing readers with an up-to-date exploration of the central issues in education today. Books in the series will examine such controversial topics as home schooling, charter schools, privatization of public schools, Native American education, African American education, literacy, curriculum development, and many others. The series is national in scope and is intended to encourage research by anyone interested in the field.

Because education is undergoing radical if not revolutionary change, the series is particularly concerned with how contemporary controversies in education affect both the organization of schools and the content and delivery of curriculum. Authors will endeavor to provide a balanced understanding of the issues and their effects on teachers, students, parents, administrators, and policymakers. The aim of the Contemporary Education Issues series is to publish excellent research on today's educational concerns by some of the finest scholar/practitioners in the field while pointing to new directions. The series promises to offer important analyses of some of the most controversial issues facing society today.

Danny Weil
Series Editor

❧ Preface

Multicultural and Diversity Education is a comprehensive reference guide to the latest trends and developments in the field. I cover wide-ranging developments in philosophy and policy through practical applications, and include recent trends in critical multiculturalism, whiteness studies, postmodern theories of identity and community, and community participation. Examples and comparisons will benefit school boards, school administrators, labor unions, community members, nonprofit organizations, parents, and teachers. This book presents choices available to educational institutions and their communities, with suggestions for how to surpass the initial steps that often alienate community members or perpetuate the problems that motivated an interest in diversity education in the first place. Difficult tasks await those who undertake the examination of their own culpability in the postcolonial legacy. Seeing conflicts as part of the democratic process, this book articulates crucial issues and decisions in curriculum, school governance, and institutional organization.

Multicultural and Diversity Education provides an overview of approaches to education for a pluralistic and democratic society, an introduction to the historical origins of diversity and multicultural education, and explanations of curricular options along with case studies, with specific attention to the potential further efforts that schools and communities face. The book includes an examination of professional and state standards and legal and political contexts. Comprehensive, annotated bibliographies of print and nonprint resources for diversity and multicultural education are also included. Finally, the book presents a glossary of terms.

I would like to thank the numerous students, colleagues, and friends whose conversations and ideas have led to my current, tentative understanding of diversity education, especially Belinda Davis, who is always challenging my narrow-minded presumptions; Noah Appelbaum, who consistently helps me recognize how behind I am in my knowledge of popular culture; Sophia Appelbaum, who reminds me every day what is really important for children; Aaron Tenenbaum, who will make a great teacher committed to social justice and democracy; Danny Weil, for his insightful help as editor and colleague in multicultural education; Jesse Naidoo and Stella Clark, for their really important questions; Rochelle Kaplan, for her brilliant comprehension of the politics of educational institutions; and Kia Karaam and Karen Mitchell, for their important help in pulling together the final manuscript. My thanks go also to Lisa Hennon, Graciela Slesaransky-Poe, Leif Gustavson, Joe Cytrynbaum, Deborah Pomeroy, Bette Goldstone, Steve Gulkus, Jeff Shultz, Christina Ager, Cindy Reedy, Anne Brown, Jane Duffy, and Steve Goldberg for their suggestions, along with the members of the Department of Education at Arcadia University for all of their trust and support. The ideas in this book originated in collaborations on the "Education in a Multicultural Society" course at the University of Michigan with Fred Goodman, Ernestine Enomoto, David Bair, David Anderson, and Mary Antony. Finally, I want to thank Alicia Merritt and Melanie Stafford for guiding last-minute decisions and keeping me to a reasonable deadline.

Peter Appelbaum

❧ Introduction

This book provides a comprehensive look at diversity and multicultural education for schools in the United States. Multiculturalism as we know it today grew out of political work in the 1960s. This legacy is both good and bad. It is good because it carries into the next century the best of the ideals and values of that historic moment. Yet, it is potentially bad not only because multiculturalism can suffer from association with the "political" or "radical" and thus be inappropriately dismissed but also because multicultural efforts run the risk of perpetuating aspects of early efforts that we now understand as poorly informed or inadequately theorized. Most of us in education believe we are multiculturalists. But because multiculturalism has occurred in versions that are offensive to many members of our community, and indeed because versions of it can actually work, ironically, against some goals of multiculturalism, this book uses "diversity education" to stand for a set of practices more fully informed by recent work in "critical multicultural education," "critical pedagogy," "cultural studies," "white studies," "identity politics," and the "economies of racism." These theoretical perspectives make their appearance as appropriate throughout the book, and will be explained in those sections of the book where they are important to understand. The book is organized around core questions, some of which are common to the Contemporary Education Issues series of reference books, and others of which are specific to the topic of diversity education.

Two themes weave the topic of multicultural and diversity education together. The first is that this kind of education is a framework for understanding and participating in the process of schooling; to think as a "multiculturalist," "pluralist," or "diversity educator" is to understand education and schooling as a social, cultural, and political activity. The second is that diversity and multicultural education should be part of and the context for *all* educational activity, not just during certain months or days of the year.

These themes suggest that multicultural and diversity education requires a reexamination of what Americans believe to be the purposes and needs of students, schools, and educational activities in general. And, although you will read in this book about some approaches to multiculturalism that add special programs or practices to the regular school day, you will find that successful diversity education for the new millennium really means changing the way administrators, teachers, and students look at each and every curricular area and the structures and policies that govern educational institutions. The book primarily focuses on nursery through secondary education, but will likely be useful to educators in other contexts as well.

Most available works in multicultural education are either very academic and thus unlikely to be read by many educators outside of the academy, or very practical and hands-on, and thus unlikely to be read by very many people who are thinking about the underlying anthropological, ethical, philosophical, and political assumptions that guide current practices. The prevailing literature mirrors the "reality" that there is little collaborative effort in educational work to inform practice with serious theory, or to have theory cowritten by practitioners.

The book you have before you is informed by my years of collaborative work with many different people in many different schools. The purpose for writing this book is to provide a common text that can be read by most members of the educational community. It is a compendium and distillation of a burgeoning market of "products" that are luring teachers to buy them and use them. How can one determine where to go or whom to believe with regard to how to define multicultural education and how to implement diversity education? The existing resource books compete with each other and jockey for prime position in the marketplace of conflicting doctrines about "what multiculturalism is." I am open to the claim that this book, too, is one more product in that market. I hope readers find this book, as part of a series dedicated to providing up-to-date explorations of central issues in education, helpful as a reference. There really are no other recent works available that focus on how contemporary controversies in education affect both the organization of schools and the everyday content and delivery of instruction.

Chapter 1 begins with an overview of multicultural education and diversity education. It introduces working definitions of multiculturalism and diversity, and discusses competing and conflicting visions for multicultural education. Political and educational arguments "for" and "against" multicultural education are examined. The chapter introduces the work of key people in the field, and attempts to distinguish between the ideas of multiculturalism, which some people now think are a bit old-fashioned, and more refined or nuanced ideas about education for cultural democracy, which people sometimes refer to as "diversity education." The overview in this first chapter is organized as if to answer someone who had asked: "What is multicultural education? Why do we have multicultural education? Why should I care about multicultural education, and what should I know about multicultural education?"

Chapter 2 sets out to answer the question, "What is the history of multicultural education?" This chapter addresses someone who wants an organized timeline of key events in the history of educational reform that they can use as a collection of benchmarks to inform their understanding of the issues. Multiculturalism, however, questions the possibility of a simple one-perspective, linear timeline of "the story" of anything. To read into the past a particular sequence of events is highly problematic. Given our topic, it is essential that we understand the historical nature of the idea of multiculturalism itself: that it grows out of a particular moment in history, and that any effort to select artifacts from before or after that "moment" is a political act. But, nevertheless, cultural democracy would claim that it is crucial for us to undertake a serious examination of the genealogy of diversity education, and to keep in mind relevant aspects of that genealogy.

Chapter 3 offers a discussion of a range of curricular approaches to multicultural and diversity education. How do these approaches respond to the conflicting and overlapping justifications and expectations that people hold for multiculturalism, given the variety of definitions and social and political contexts presented in Chapters 1 and 2? Equity issues; student, teacher, family, administrator, and community frustrations; and the dilemmas of assessment and classroom management are highlighted as potentially useful or misleading in the establishment of successful school programs. This chapter juxtaposes practical suggestions for curriculum implementation. It presents important ideas about critical multiculturalism, arguing that only a "critical pedagogy for diversity" can address throughout the school curriculum the problems of simplistic approaches to identity and the ways that consumer culture makes the transformation of society so difficult. One important aspect of both consumer culture and school curricula is the way that they provide images, actions, and texts that stand for other things, texts, actions, and so on. This process of "representation" creates the impression that there are easily understood and simple truths by which we can interpret the world. Critical pedagogy for diversity, I suggest, explicitly studies the politics of education and the politics of representations in the curriculum and in popular culture; critical multiculturalism makes all of this a part of educating for a democracy.

Chapter 4 provides case studies of multicultural and diversity education. How do some people try to "do" multiculturalism? Given the questions that critical multiculturalism raises regarding representation, it is difficult to represent school programs as simple stories. To do so would "essentialize" cultural elements, assuming fundamentally un-changeable categories of reality. Instead, each unique story serves as an example of the ideological perspective of the approach and simultane-ously as an "untelling" of the essentializing narratives of cultural and other identities. This was a hard chapter to write because, even though I know a lot of people who do great things in so many fantastic schools, it is hard to profile what might be called a "success." The "best" schools are in the midst of ongoing discussion and debate about whether what they are doing has merit in the first place. These schools are a model of cultural democracy. At the same time, the current discourse of educa-tional reform does not support serious attention to diversity education, and instead redirects our attention to forms of evaluation that under-mine many goals of multiculturalism. Educators tend to think of multi-culturalism as something that was "solved" a decade or two ago (for such educators, multiculturalism appeared on the scene as a problem they had to address; they were told that their curricula needed to be more multicultural, which became one more issue in a relentless chain of problems to deal with—thus, administrators and teachers sought simple, short-term prescriptions). For these reasons, most efforts in multicultural education are still in the process of growing and moving away from the more offensive versions toward the more progressive and productive visions that people hold. The stories in this chapter are valu-able for the variety of contexts and for their range of approaches to sys-temic change.

Chapter 5 addresses questions about the political and legal issues that might be relevant to multicultural and diversity education. Because multiculturalism demands a personal and collective reexamination of our beliefs about democracy, equity, rights, and social justice in general, this chapter offers the interesting perspective that identity, diversity, and citizenship are intertwined in our assumptions about the way schools and other educational institutions need to operate. State, local, and national frameworks and standards provide a curious legal back-drop to the discussion. On the one hand, these documents can be used as legal justification for many reform efforts in diversity education. On the other hand, from a multicultural perspective, they seem to ignore the important issues of diversity and equity. How does an educator ne-gotiate this terrain? Challenges include the role of high-stakes testing, the effective support of unions and professional associations, and the conviction to address issues of multiculturalism in the current political and legal climate.

Chapter 6 provides one last look at serious barriers to multicul-turalism. Why, I ask, do we not see more examples of the kinds of programs profiled in Chapter 4? Because, I believe, too many people are attached to traditions and expectations common to the ways in which we group students, recruit and train teachers, interpret our school culture, and adhere to policies of school governance. Each traditional set of relationships among curricula, practitioners, students, families, and community members sets up criteria for judging the legitimacy of institutional structures, "common sense" expectations about what teaching and learning are supposed to look like, and particular roles for certain members of the school community in decision-making and policy-setting processes.

Chapter 6 ends with a set of questions for the reader, designed to challenge our idea of the purpose of a reference book in a critical multicultural democracy. If we are to create a cultural democracy, we need to question the role of the question. In doing so, I model one version of education for cultural democracy, a version that values the articulation of questions, rather than the synthesis of information, as the final "product." This form of education moves us away from a problem-solving orientation to multicultural schooling and toward a problem-*posing* approach. In critical multicultural education, participants shun the essentializing tendencies of solutions in favor of new inquiries and the challenge of change.

Chapter 7 lists selected organizations that help multicultural and diversity educators. Chapter 8 provides both print and nonprint resources as well as a collection of materials that can be helpful as "talking points" at meetings of educators, community members, and others interested in further exploring diversity education.

The key thing to keep in mind throughout this book is that the United States is a crucible for "postcolonial" politics and culture. Fears, fantasies, conflicts, and celebrations reflect the kinds of experiences and standpoints that continue to express response to the forms of economic, racial, ethnic, and geographic inequality and domination achieved through the historical period when European colonial powers established their colonies. Schools are always important sites of social conflict. They always will be. That is part of the intellectual excitement of working with educational institutions. So we must recognize that schools are always "successful" in accomplishing what they do in fact "accomplish"—those schools or students who are described as "failing" are in fact "succeeding at failure." The implications of this for a diverse, democratic society are obvious to multicultural educators. There is no escape from the history of education in North America, which includes domination of colonized people, segregation by race, class, gender, religion, and other categories of difference, and economic and political injustice. Multicultural education is not simply about declaring that we all will get along. It is more about the courage to confront our own fears and fantasies. It is centrally about achieving the will to work for social change, and to hold out the hope that everyday work on collaboration and democracy can be part of the possibilities.

Peter Appelbaum

Chapter One

⚭ Overview

This chapter provides an overview of multicultural and diversity education, with attention to current working definitions of multiculturalism and diversity, competing and conflicting visions for multicultural education, and political and educational arguments "for" and "against" multicultural education. The discussion introduces the ideas of key people working in the field and distinguishes between the ideas of multiculturalism, which some people now think are a bit old-fashioned, and more refined or nuanced ideas about education for cultural democracy, which people sometimes refer to as "diversity education."

WHAT IS MULTICULTURAL
AND DIVERSITY EDUCATION?

Christine Sleeter once opened a delightful collection of writing on multicultural education that she edited, *Empowerment Through Multicultural Education* (1991), with a brief story about an urban elementary principal expressing skepticism toward her interests in multicultural education. This principal argued that, given all of the problems and difficulties that low-income students and students of color face, it would be far better to promote the effective schools movement or programs for at-risk students.

Similarly, the American Educational Research Association once featured on their Web site a streaming video of a session from their 1999 annual conference that raised controversial questions about social and cultural responses to current educational issues. Alfie Kohn spoke against high-stakes testing, punishment and reward systems of discipline, and drill and practice curricula; several other researchers confirmed that changes in educational practices away from these techniques and toward culturally sensitive and meaning-based practices had led in their experience to significant improvements. However, an

1

important respondent at this session declared that the other researchers had no understanding of the realities that the students she worked with in the Chicago public schools had to face in their lives. It was one thing to say that standardized tests do not reflect conceptual understanding and problem-solving skills, she said, but it is another thing to deny her students a chance to demonstrate that they can excel as much as any other child on these tests. She pointedly noted that her students would never be given the chance to impress somebody with their higher-level thinking skills unless they first got high scores on these seemingly meaningless tests.

What we find is that different people interpret their lives and the lives of others in very different ways. But this does not mean that we should just sit back and say that because there are many different opinions, we cannot solve problems of inequity. Indeed, this is what generally goes on in schools: because there are conflicts over what multicultural education is, and more profoundly over what society is or could be, now or in the future, or even what a person or a child is, we often decide that we cannot really deal with such issues.

In fact, the whole notion of a common school, which grew out of the work of Horace Mann and others in the mid-nineteenth century, intentionally has built into it the idea that controversial issues should be kept out of the common school. In this view, the school should be a place where the things on which we agree are emphasized and understood. Schooling, in this view of education, is a community-building and bridge-building institution, a patriotic institution. And of course schools do serve these important functions. But we also need to recognize that this way of understanding schooling also brings with it a way of ignoring important conflicts—sweeping them under the rug—only to have them surface in more serious ways in other contexts.

Some people have suggested that multicultural and diversity education is a form of cooptation of minority or disempowered peoples into the system, rather than of challenging white racism. Indeed, this book refers to "diversity education" specifically to avoid the increasingly common critiques of multiculturalism that characterize it, regardless of the particular version, as trying to make everyone alike rather than addressing issues of diversity and difference, social inequality, and the need for social change. Multiculturalism in this cartoonish interpretation becomes an "accommodation strategy for defusing anger brought about by oppression" (Sleeter 1991, 6). It is easy to see that there has been a consistent attempt on the part of schools in the United States in the last couple of centuries to "Americanize" people by making them conform to the dominant white culture.

Others portray multiculturalism as a way for affluent suburban kids to be taught how to accept their lucky set of privileges. In mostly white, mostly comfortable, and caring schools, these critics report, it is easy to say that all people are equal regardless of color, or that where one lives does not make one's character. Yet it is another thing for these privileged students to comprehend how their comfortable lifestyle depends on the oppression of others. There is an apocryphal story of a college professor who brought a gun into his sociology course to make a point. Comparing the circumstances of privilege that led his students to a college class with the situations of child abuse in sweatshops, underpaid migrant workers, Third World debt, and early death of many people, he was shocked to hear his students easily dismiss this inequity as simply the "way the world works," and state that they were just glad to be part of the lucky few that had the privileges. This professor asked for volunteers to "shoot" the gun at a teaching assistant as a symbol of the causes of early death for others, and actually found volunteers. Critics of schooling say that such uncritical attitudes at the college level grow out of the practices and structures of earlier schooling and are further reinforced at the college level.

Michael Olneck described multicultural education in an issue of the *American Educational Research Journal* as a "multifaceted movement that encompasses a wide range of ideas, purposes, practices, and communities of discourse and interest" (2000, 317). Yet he noted that multicultural education can be understood in its political origins, in the writings of theorists, and in the practices of its most loyal proponents, to be committed to resisting and displacing Euro-American cultural domination of schooling. I am not sure that we can go so far: critics use as examples people who think they are "doing multiculturalism" when they set up international food fairs or attend cultural sensitivity workshops, which can reduce multiculturalism to "Let's all get along." Indeed, for many schools, "Can't we find a way to get along with each other?" is the immediate crisis out of which an interest in multiculturalism may develop.

Nevertheless, Olneck provides an important point for us to consider. Diversity education needs to integrate content and perspectives originating in the experiences of nondominant racial, ethnic, and linguistic groups into the curriculum. Diversity education enables students to recognize the role of power in the construction of knowledge. Diversity education embraces the cultivation of democratic attitudes, values, and behaviors among students and staff. Diversity education reconceives pedagogy through its commitments. And diversity education "reorders the schools' status and cultural systems," writes Olneck, "to make them fair to those previously disempowered by Euro-American dominance" (2000, 318). Implementation of multicultural and diversity education, however, remains challenged by political, institutional, and ideological forces and constraints that tend to work against change in general, but also are often implicated in the perpetuation of inequality that multiculturalism and a commitment to diversity strive to undermine.

Mara Sapon-Shevin, in *Because We Can Change the World* (1999), asks "what does it mean for a school or a classroom to be a community? What are the characteristics that define community and what are the values that might be central organizing forces in those communities?" (1). She calls us to respond to increasing recognition of the importance of developing respect for human dignity, for teaching students to be active participants, both in their own education and in the community. George Wood, in an *Educational Leadership* article on "Teaching for Democracy," finds that schools that have a vision of students as citizens give their students a sense of community that helps them make a connection with the world. Eric Schaps argues in an article appearing in *Social Studies Review* that all aspects of students' development—intellectual, social, and moral—can best be fostered through the creation of caring classroom communities. He asserts that teaching students to be socially responsible must be anchored in the development of deeply personal commitments to such core values as justice, tolerance, and concern for others. In inaugurating a series of monographs in 1995 sponsored by the National Council of Teachers of Mathematics on equity in mathematics education, Walter Secada, Elizabeth Fennema, and Lisa Byrd Adajian appreciate the ongoing work in the areas of differential student achievement, course-taking and careers, tracking, and teacher-student interactions. But these scholars see the challenge in terms of more recent developments that make problematic such classically held notions as race, gender, social class, and even the goals of schooling itself. Key to reform in mathematics education, as in other areas of education, they say, are poststructural analyses and semiotics, the incorporation of a range of perspectives and voices that have been previously unheard, and new kinds of questions from different points of view.

COMPETING AND CONFLICTING VISIONS FOR MULTICULTURAL EDUCATION

Common classifications of types of multicultural education have been described in the literature by James Banks and Christine Sleeter. Banks couched his ideas in terms of how multicultural content is integrated into the curriculum (see Table 1.1); Sleeter, in her attempt to understand how people could have such drastically different ideas about multicultural education, offered an analysis of the differences (see Table 1.2). Each establishes a hierarchy in which higher categories of multiculturalism incorporate and improve upon lower categories. Both sets of categories are useful to this day.

Banks—Integrating Multicultural Content

James Banks's categories almost read as a list of steps that schools can take to introduce multiculturalism into their classroom practices. The danger of this interpretation, however, is that the first couple of categories have a number of negative implications that should be avoided if at all possible. The first, the contributions approach, asks teachers to find some way to expose their students to ethnic, racial, gender, religious, or other diversity in their curricular content. One way to do this is to designate certain activities at a special time, such as reading about women leaders during Women's History Month (March) or researching African American scientists for African American History Month (February). Some schools hold ethnic food festivals to celebrate the diversity of their community. All of these ideas, however, unfortunately promote a superficial understanding of ethnicity in general and of particular cultures, and give the direct impression that the content is not important because it is not part of the "real," regular curriculum. These practices can reinforce implicit conceptions that ethnicities are "outside the mainstream" rather than focusing on the local community as inherently multicultural. For example, an international food fair telegraphs the "foreign" status of many cultures, rather than helping students to learn about the diverse foods that are part of the local community, all of which could be called "American." The result is often a stereotyping of "others." Another common problem with this approach is that it relies on the contributions of people in the community, many of whom do not feel comfortable sharing information about the communities of which they are a part. An administrator or teacher may feel self-righteous inviting families to come into the school and share stories about religious observances or special foods; the family members, meanwhile, may resent how little the school knows about their life and culture, and see the invitation as an insult.

The additive approach requires the school and teachers to research and learn about multicultural content. Implicit in this approach is enough respect for cultural differences to take on the responsibility of personally learning about them and making them a part of the curricu-

Table 1.1 Approaches to Multicultural Education (James Banks)

APPROACH: Contributions

Description
Heroes, cultural components, holidays, and other discrete elements related to ethnic groups are added to the curriculum on special days, occasions, and for special celebrations.

Examples
Famous African Americans are studied during African American History Month.
Famous Mexican Americans are studied on *Cinco de Mayo.*
Diwali and *Kwanzaa* are studied around Christmas, but Hindu and African American cultures are rarely studied at other times of the year.
Ethnic foods are studied with little attention to the cultures in which the foods are embedded.

Pros
Quick and easy way to put ethnic content into the curriculum with little controversy.
Gives high visibility to ethnic heroes alongside commonly known mainstream heroes.
Commonly done by teachers and educators, so easily understood and implemented.

Cons
Superficial understanding of ethnic cultures.
Gives impression that content is unimportant because it is not part of the "real" curriculum.
Reinforces stereotypes and misconceptions.
Can reinforce impression that ethnicities are "outside the mainstream" rather than focusing on the local community as inherently multicultural.
Mainstream criteria are used to select heroes and cultural elements, delegitimizing alternative perspectives.

APPROACH: Additive

Description
Content, concepts, themes, and perspectives are added to the curriculum without changing the structure.

Examples
Read a book by Toni Morrison in a literature unit without reconceptualizing the unit or giving students the background knowledge to understand the book.
Play *mancala* or *dreidel* in math class without discussing the mathematics of the game or using the game as a vehicle for learning important mathematics.
Add a unit on Japanese internment to U.S. history without treating the Japanese in any other unit.
Leave the core curriculum intact, but add a course on ethnic studies or racism and sexism.

Pros
Easy way to add ethnic content to the curriculum without changing the structure (which requires substantial curriculum changes and staff development).

Can be implemented within the existing curriculum structure.

Cons

Indirectly teaches that ethnic history and content are not integral to the curriculum.

Students are taught to view ethnic groups from an Anglo or Euro-centric perspective.

Fails to help students understand how the dominant culture and ethnic cultures are interconnected and interrelated.

APPROACH: Transformation

Description

Curricular goals and structures are changed to enable students to view concepts, events, issues, problems, and themes from the perspectives of diverse cultural, ethnic, racial, and other groups.

Students attend group facilitation workshops, learn how to play the guitar and lead groups of people in sing-alongs; how to put together a Web-based presentation for the city council.

Examples

American Revolution unit describes the meaning of the revolution to Anglo loyalists, African Americans, Native Americans, and the British.

A literature unit includes works by William Faulkner, Joyce Carol Oates, Langston Hughes, N. Scott Momaday, Saul Bellow, Maxine Hong Kingston, Rudolfo Anaya, and Piri Thomas.

A unit on classification of organisms applies Native American and other classification schemes in addition to mainstream "Western" science categories.

Pros

Enables students to understand the complex ways in which the diverse racial and cultural groups participated in the formation of U.S. society and culture.

Helps reduce racial and ethnic encapsulation.

Enables diverse ethnic, racial, and religious groups to see their cultures, ethos, and perspectives in the school curriculum.

Gives students a balanced view of the nature and development of U.S. culture and society.

Helps to empower victimized racial, ethnic, and religious groups.

Cons

Requires substantial curriculum revision, in-service training, and the identification and development of materials written from the varying perspectives.

Staff development for the institutionalization of this approach must be continual and ongoing.

Some people fear such substantial changes to the curriculum, claiming a "dumbing down" of the curriculum, or that the curriculum will result in reduced attention to expected content for later career and life opportunities.

Table 1.1 *continued*

APPROACH: Social Action

Description
Students study social change and social organizing skills and effect change in their community as part of the curriculum.

Examples
While researching the emergence and implementation of child labor laws in the United States, students and teachers organize local alternatives to purchasing clothing made by child labor in sweatshops, and begin to research the opportunities for affecting migrant farm workers' rights in the United States.

Pros
The only truly democratic education for democracy.
Likely to make a difference in the lives of students and the community, increasing student engagement and performance as well as family and community involvement.

Cons
Likely to elicit direct hostility as a nonconventional approach despite the efficacy.
When directly implemented or even discussed, it is likely to be labeled dangerous or "too political."

lum. Nevertheless, this kind of curriculum continues to project diversity as not really part of the mainstream curriculum (in fact, the structure of the curriculum can end up implicitly teaching students that such knowledge is clearly of lesser value just by the way the material is integrated into the curriculum); such a curriculum is delivered from an Anglo or European perspective and fails to enable students to develop an understanding of how dominant and nondominant cultures are interrelated and interconnected.

In the transformation approach, curricular goals and structures are changed to enable students to view concepts, events, issues, problems, and themes from the perspectives of diverse cultural, ethnic, racial, and other groups. This helps reduce racial and ethnic encapsulation and enables diverse ethnic, racial, and religious groups to see their cultures, ethos, and perspectives in the school curriculum. It also helps to empower victimized racial, ethnic, and religious groups.

Finally, the social action approach explicitly prepares students to act in response to the issues out of which the need for multicultural education grows: injustice, inequity, intergroup conflict, and the legacies of oppression. Students study social change and social organizing skills as an overarching focus of their curriculum, and effect change in their community as part of this curriculum.

Table 1.2 More Approaches to Multicultural Education (Christine Sleeter)

APPROACH: Human Relations

Description

Students and staff work together to improve interactions and relationships between and among members of various ethnic, racial, religious, and other groups.

Examples

In-service trains teachers to understand that some Asian American children avoid eye contact as a sign of respect for teachers, not as a technique of disrespect.

Teachers and volunteer parents talk with students about how some Latina students accomplish more in small groups because they can avoid making their peers look stupid by standing out themselves in class.

Pros

Generally received as positive and nonthreatening. Easy to implement within existing structure of in-service and professional development.

Interpersonal skills are often easily learned.

Cons

Hides serious ethnic, racial, religious, and other conflicts.

Does not respond to most multicultural and diversity concerns.

APPROACH: Teaching the Exceptional and Culturally Different

Description

School responds to special needs of students from varying groups.

Examples

Special after-school sessions are scheduled to help Creole-speaking students with math and science.

High-achievers are separated from low-achievers in order to provide extra help to the low-achievers.

Spanish-first-language students are encouraged to work together in math class before presenting their ideas in English to the rest of the class, in order to help them develop the concepts in their first language.

Pros

Easy to implement within the existing structure.

Requires no changes to the existing curriculum or teaching practices in the classroom. Can lead to significant gains in test scores and other indicators if targeted toward such goals.

Cons

Perpetuates a "blame-the-victim" mentality, in which a medical model places students in the hands of experts who diagnose special needs and recommend prescriptions for meeting those needs. This disempowers students and their families.

Ignores students' strengths (including what they bring with them from outside school), motives, goals, insights, strategies for learning, or personal identities that give direction to their growth.

Table 1.2 *continued*

APPROACH: Multicultural Education (Cultural Democracy)

Description

Curriculum and organization are changed using ideas from Banks and others to facilitate a community of teachers and learners in the school.

Classrooms and schools are redesigned to model an unoppressive, equal society that is also culturally diverse.

Examples

Thematic units are planned collaboratively among the teachers to integrate all curricular content. At all times in the process, the planners ask themselves if they have found ways to respond to multicultural and diversity issues in terms of content, structure, student participation, and community involvement.

Teachers and aides are hired with important attention to cultural diversity.

Pros

Like Banks's "Transformation" approach, students are enabled to see themselves and others as parts of overlapping and crucial contributors to the development of society and knowledge about society, to recognize the role of power in defining knowledge, and to understand the content from multiple and varying perspectives. Students are empowered as individuals by achieving and receiving validation for who they are, and are empowered for social change by having lived a pluralist model.

Cons

Requires substantial curriculum revision, in-service training, and the identification and development of materials written from the varying perspectives.

Staff development for the institutionalization of this approach must be continual and ongoing.

Some people fear such substantial changes to the curriculum, claiming a "dumbing down" of the curriculum, or that the curriculum will result in re-duced attention to expected content for later career and life opportunities.

APPROACH: Single Group Studies

Description

A particular social group, for example, Chicano or gay and lesbian Ameri-cans, are studied in detail, understanding the entire curriculum from the perspective of this group.

Examples

Black studies, Chicano studies, women's studies, which explicitly teach students about the history of the target group's oppression and how oppres-sion works today, as well as the culture the group has developed within op-pressive circumstances.

Pros

More than any other approach, this one promotes identification with and solidarity among members of the specific ethnic or gender target group, clearly defining boundaries between the in-group and out-groups.

More likely to promote intergroup understanding than superficial curric-ular structures and approaches.

Curricula exist and can de identified, with effort.

Table 1.2 *continued*

Cons

Triggers strongly negative political arguments, including the notion that it fosters divisiveness and reinforces difference rather than working toward harmony.

Fewer available resources for integrating mathematical and scientific content than for history, social studies, literature, and the arts.

Hard for supporters of a traditional disciplinary approach to comprehend.

APPROACH: Education that is Multicultural and Social Reconstructionist
Description

Students and teachers together take on social action projects, work to improve their community as a multicultural democracy, and develop social change and leadership skills.

Examples

After making a list of possible actions that they could take regarding the issues studied in the unit (including no actions), students consider the possible consequences of each of the identified actions. Projects grow out of the ensuing discussion.

Pros

Forges a coalition among various oppressed groups as well as members of dominant groups, teaching directly about political and economic oppression and discrimination, and preparing young people directly in social action skills.

Cons

So radically different from most people's expectations for school that we have trouble finding any support and models, outside of unions, community, and church groups that are not normally labeled "school."

Christine Sleeter—Cultural/Organizational Approaches

Sleeter (1991) describes the human relations approach as aiming toward sensitivity training and teaching that "we are all the same because we are all different" (11). Advocates talk about the power of love, unity, and harmony, and of the need for individuals to try to change the attitudes and behaviors of other individuals who thwart harmonious interactions. Unfortunately, as she notes, many people identify this approach with multicultural education when there are at least four other ways to understand work with pluralism and diversity. In the *teaching-the-exceptional-and-culturally-different* approach, educators try to raise the achievement of students of color mainly through designing culturally compatible educational programs. By obtaining skills and capabilities, this approach argues, the student will be able to succeed. The key to academic success, in this way of understanding schools, is to assist students in the internalization of mainstream cultural values embedded in our school system through meaningful and culturally appropriate relationships. This approach assumes that society is sufficiently open so that once this mainstreaming occurs, individuals will "make it." It also devalues cultural differences and ignores conflicts with the mainstream values and dispositions, but, more importantly, delegitimizes alternative ways of knowing and approaches to learning.

Advocates of Sleeter's other three approaches stress the need to help students acquire basic academic skills and to develop understanding of their own background as well as that of other groups in society. But equally important is helping them to develop a vision of a better society and to acquire the knowledge and skills necessary to bring about constructive social change. They all conceptualize empowerment of students and faculty as collective social action in addition to achievement.

The *multicultural education/cultural democracy* approach attempts to redesign classrooms and schools to model an unoppressive, equal, and pluralistic society that is culturally diverse. By having lived the experience, students develop many of the human relations and academic skills, but are also prepared to enact the kind of social justice action that they experience in school.

The *single group studies* approach effectively works against the negative aspects of other curricular models by avoiding stereotyping and superficial study in favor of in-depth, long-term understanding of a particular cultural, ethnic, or other perspective.

The *multicultural and reconstructionist* approach uses all of the above strategies within the context of developing social change skills and projects, forging intergroup coalitions, teaching directly about political and economic oppression and discrimination, and preparing its students through social action projects to take leadership in their community.

POLITICAL AND EDUCATIONAL ARGUMENTS "FOR" AND "AGAINST" MULTICULTURAL EDUCATION

Mara Sapon-Shevin (1999) frames diversity education as a new definition of *civics:* those skills, attitudes, and beliefs needed to be a member of a community (see Table 1.3 for an outline). She proposes that a new civics curriculum would help us to shape classrooms, schools, and societies that value community. Learning to be part of that community, she writes, is an essential, perhaps *the* essential goal we should set for students and ourselves. As long we resist the temptation to reduce this to something outside of the curriculum, and instead understand such an approach as embedded in all of our classroom practices, curricular

Table 1.3 CIVICS

C	Courage
I	Inclusion
V	Value
I	Integrity
C	Cooperation
S	Safety

structures, school policies, and community involvement, I suggest we can take Sapon-Shevin's new definition as a useful argument for how crucial such education is for a democracy.

Courage, for Sapon-Shevin, is "what it takes when a person leaves behind something he or she knows well and embraces (even tentatively) something unknown or frightening"—to let go of the familiar and do things differently (2). *Inclusion* means that we all belong. It "means not having to fight for a chance to be part of a classroom or school community" (4); it means all students and staff are accepted. This is different from mainstreaming or integration because it brings with it the understanding that there is a presumption of inclusion. The key here is that it is not up to the child or his or her family but up to the school to make inclusion possible. *Value* represents the idea of "valuing every individual without reference to the value of any other individual" (7). Value means working against the predisposition to devalue some people, and also against the systematic instruction in ranking people according to set criteria. *Integrity* speaks to wholeness, to creating the sense of trust and security necessary for people to be their whole selves and share their whole selves with the other members of the community. In the ideal school, there would not have to be lies or secrets about who we are; we would "show ourselves fully, knowing that we would be accepted in our complexity, accepted even with our seeming contradictions and inadequacies" (8). *Cooperation* means "people working together to achieve a common goal, supporting and helping one another along the way" (11). This means working against forms of competition that devalue others. *Safety* means every kind of safety required for people to work together and learn. This includes attention to physical safety. But it also means establishing an environment in which students and staff are confident that they will not be hit, hurt, or physically threatened or abused in any way. It means "emotional safety, the safety to be oneself, to be vulnerable, to ask for help, and to be warmly supported" (13). Surely we can support such aims as consistent with an understanding of civics. But to act on these aims is another thing. This book is a contribution to helping you to do this.

There are concrete reasons for the need to implement multicultural and diversity education. The population of the United States is rapidly becoming more racially and ethnically diverse. In 2000, the U.S. Bureau of the Census reported the U.S. population was 12.91 percent African American, 11.42 percent Hispanic, 4.09 percent Asian or Pacific Islander, 0.87 percent Native American (including Eskimo or Aleut), and 82.12 percent non-Hispanic white (see Table 1.4). In the 1980s six million immigrants joined the U.S. population. Most immigrants are from areas other than Europe. About 43 percent of the Hispanic population immigrated in the 1970s and 1980s, and fully 70 percent of the Asian population immigrated during those two decades. This diversity certainly provides a richer pool of cultural resources in the United States, while at the same time increasing the possibility for misunderstanding and resentment.

More to the point, the increasing racial diversity of the United States demands that the nation come to terms with racism. Waves of white European immigrants blended in with the dominant population after a generation or two. Non-Europeans continue to be visibly distinct; this perpetuates racism and a loss of the optimism associated with immigration. There is also a long history of nondominant groups in North America who have experienced discrimination and oppression throughout their history, including Chicanos or Mexican Americans, Puerto Ricans, Native Americans, and African Americans.

The persistence of discrimination and oppression undermines any sense that improved racial attitudes can be noted as a sign of progress. In 1963, when a Gallup poll asked whites if they would move out of their neighborhood if a black family moved next door to them, 45 percent said they would. According to a 1990 Gallup poll, only 5 percent responded in the affirmative when asked the same question. What does this mean? Perhaps it points to a discomfort with admitting to racist values in public, but not to addressing the underlying issues. A contrasting Gallup and Hugick poll in 1990 reported no significant change since the late 1970s in public opinion about African Americans' success in achieving equal opportunities. The perception of how African Americans are treated in their communities has not improved since the 1970s. There are more and more reports of a fundamental gap in how whites and blacks perceive racism and equity in the United States.

People of color continue to experience poverty and unemployment disproportionately. In 1994, whites suffered unemployment rates of 5.3 percent, Hispanics 9.9 percent, and blacks 11.5 percent. Data on Native Americans, reported less systematically, still show devastating poverty and unemployment—in 1980 the poverty rate for Native Amer-

**Table 1.4 Diversity of the U.S. Population According to
the U.S. Bureau of the Census**

Year	African American	Asian or Pacific Islander	Native American, Eskimo, or Aleut	Hispanic Origin	Non-Hispanic White
1980	11.78	1.65	0.63	6.45	85.95
1998	12.74	3.89	0.87	11.56	82.50
2000	12.91	4.09	0.87	11.42	82.12
2010 (projection)	13.47	5.13	0.93	13.82	80.48
2025 (projection)	14.19	6.56	0.99	17.59	78.23

**Table 1.5 Earnings of Full-Time Year-Round Workers
25 Years and Older (1989)**

Racial Group	Four Years High High School	1–3 Years College	4 or more Years College
White	$24,755	29,498	43,314
Black	19,813	22,813	32,046
Latino	20,567	25,620	38,559

icans was 27.5 percent overall, and 51.4 percent and 52.4 percent respectively on the Rosebud and Navajo reservations.

Studies show that black youths are staying in school longer and joining the military in greater numbers, thus no longer having an ironic "head start" on the job market for unskilled or semiskilled work. Worsening labor force statistics for black youths do not indicate increasing racial inequality but instead persistent racial inequities previously hidden by race differences in other aspects of young adulthood (see Table 1.5).

As a result of differential access to jobs, housing, health insurance, and educational institutions, estimates of quality of life in general vary according to race. Life expectancies are also different. African Americans die younger than white people, according to a recent study. People of color are more likely to be imprisoned. People of color are disenfranchised politically. Women are still subordinate to men according to many criteria such as pay equity and political representation. Although many gay, lesbian, bisexual, and transgendered youth find little conflict in terms of their own sexual orientations, others are not so fortunate. Overall, gay, lesbian, bisexual, and transgendered youth compare favorably with heterosexually identified adolescents in regard to "resilience," "reactions to distress," or "insecurities." Yet a well-known study from 1989 cited gay and lesbian youth as two to three times more likely to commit suicide, making up as much as 30 percent of all youth suicides. More recent studies confirm the high level of suicide risk, or indicate gay, lesbian, bisexual, and transgendered youth as more likely to use and abuse drugs, become victims of violence and harassment, and get thrown out of their homes to end up on the street ("GLBT Youth at Risk"; "Youth OUTreach").

The United States continues to maintain strong social class stratification. There are tremendous inequities in the distribution of wealth. Between 1978 and 1986 the middle class shrank and the lower class grew more than twice as much as the upper class in numbers. Many who have jobs are employed for less than a full day's work or for only part of the year. In addition to the number of men and women who are officially recorded as unemployed, at least an equal number have given up the search. Despite the myth that anyone who desires it can attain wealth, Jencks (1990) found occupation to be predicted largely by educational attainment, which in turn is predicted by family socioeconomic background. In other words, children tend to grow up and occupy the same social class position as their parents. Even among those with the same level of education, the children of wealthier parents are much more likely to attain high-paying jobs than are children of lower- or middle-class parents. Those controlling the greatest proportion of wealth tend to have the most political power. For example, those most likely to sit on state and local boards, boards of regents for colleges and universities, and boards of corporations are from the upper socioeconomic classes and make the rules by which society operates.

Finally, those with disabilities constitute a subordinate group, although it is harder to find statistics. The exclusion of significant numbers of students with disabilities from both state and national data collection programs and/or nonexistent disability-specific variables used to identify these students in these programs makes it all but impossible to describe the status of students with disabilities (McGrew et al. 1995). Although the graduation rates for students with disabilities has risen steadily since 1993, and while the dropout rate has declined, the dropout rate was still 28.9 percent in 1999. Although rates differed by categories of types of disability, students identified with "emotional disturbance" experienced a 50 percent dropout rate; those with visual impairments experienced a 12 percent dropout rate. Dropout rates for Hispanic and black students with disabilities were, respectively, 34 and 32 percent; rates for American Indian/Alaska native students were as high as 44 percent (Office of Special Education Programs 2001). Americans with disabilities are less than half as likely as their nondisabled counterparts to own a computer, and they are about one-quarter as likely to use the Internet (Kaye 2000).

Standards-based reform has generated new challenges for special education. The idea that students with disabilities should be held to the same standards and tests as other students, and that schools should prepare students to meet these goals, presents a strong message. But requirements that link promotion and graduation to high-stakes testing could harm students with disabilities. Those working in the field of special education are beginning to explain what they believe is needed in terms of academic support and professional development for special education and regular education teachers, as well as the variety of interventions required for enabling students to meet these goals. Complicating work with students who have disabilities are the complexity and quantity of paperwork required by the IDEA (Individuals with Disabilities Education Act); educators spend an enormous amount of time demonstrating their compliance with the law, responding to legal contestations, and even interpreting their own assessment of whether or not they understand the details of the law (American Youth Policy Forum 2002).

Students with disabilities are less likely than their nondisabled counterparts to participate in a full academic curriculum. Students with disabilities achieve at lower levels in comparison with their nondisabled counterparts. There is a consistent overrepresentation of African American students in special education. African American and American Indian/Native American students are, respectively, 15 percent and 1.3 percent of the special education population, whereas only 1 percent of the general population is typically referred to special education. Whereas 2.2 percent of African American students are identified as mentally retarded, only 0.8 percent of white students are similarly identified. And, while Hispanic students are represented in special education at about the same rate as their representation in the general population, white and Asian students are underrepresented in special education by comparison with their percentage of the general population. Young people with disabilities are less likely to enroll in postsecondary education. And adults with disabilities are less likely to be employed. Fifty percent of adults with disabilities were employed in 1997 as compared with 84 percent of nondisabled adults. Median earnings for disabled employed adults were $17,700 as compared with $23,700 for nondisabled adults.

Statistics are dangerous because they can be misinterpreted as indicating signs of weakness within a particular group. That is not what is intended here. Diversity educators recognize the legacy of discrimination and oppression in these statistics. The picture is one of increasing diversity but also increasing disparity. According to the Children's Defense Fund, every day 2,833 children drop out of school; 6 children commit suicide; 1,407 babies are born to teen mothers; 100,000 children are homeless. Every 34 seconds, a baby is born to a mother who did not graduate from high school; every 25 seconds a baby is born into poverty; every 2 hours, a child or youth is killed by firearms.

What are the implications for education? Educators have been tempted at times to say "this is why we cannot do very much in the schools. Don't expect too much given all of the problems." A more ethical response would be to ask what those involved with young people can understand about the lives of the young people they work with. A seemingly simple idea is to take the experiences of youth into consideration in the design and assessment of educational programs, policies, and possibilities.

REFERENCES AND FURTHER READING

American Youth Policy Forum. 2002. *Educating Children with Disabilities: The Good News and the Work Ahead.* Washington, DC: American Youth Policy Forum and the Center on Education Policy.

Banks, James, and Cherry McGee Banks, eds. 2000. *Multicultural Education: Issues and Perspectives.* New York: John Wiley and Sons.

Children's Defense Fund. 2001. *The State of America's Children Yearbook.* Washington, DC: Children's Defense Fund.

Gay, Geneva, and James Banks. 2000. *Culturally Responsive Teaching: Theory, Research and Practice.* New York: Teachers College Press.

"GLBT Youth at Risk." Available at 10th Muse Web site, http://www.pflagreno.org/safeschools/atrisk.html.

Jencks, Christopher. 1990. *The Urban Underclass.* Washington, DC: Brookings Institution.

Kaye, Stephen. 2000. *Disability and the Digital Divide.* Washington, DC: Disability Statistics Center.

McGrew, Kevin, et al. 1995. *Why We Can't Say Much about the Status of Students with Disabilities during Education Reform.* Minneapolis, MN: National Center on Educational Outcomes.

Office of Special Education Programs. 2001. *To Assure the Free Public Education of All Children with Disabilities.* Washington, DC: Office of Special Education Programs. Available at http://www.ed.gov/offices/OSERS/OSEP/Products/OSEP2001AnlRpt/index.html.

Olneck, Michael. 2000. "Can Multicultural Education Change What Counts as Cultural Capital?" *American Educational Research Journal* 37, no. 2: 317–348.

Sapon-Shevin, Mara. 1999. *Because We Can Change the World: A Practical Guide to Building Cooperative, Inclusive Classroom Communities.* Boston: Allyn & Bacon.

Schaps, Eric. 1997. "A Key Condition for Character Development: Building a Sense of Community in School." *Social Studies Review* 37, no. 1: 85–90.

Secada, Walter, Elizabeth Fennema, and Lisa Byrd Adajian, eds. 1995. *New Directions for Equity in Mathematics Education.* New York: Cambridge University Press.

Sleeter, Christine. 1991. *Empowerment Through Multicultural Education.* Albany, NY: State University of New York Press.

Sleeter, Christine, and Carl Grant. 1998. *Turning on Learning: Five Approaches for Multicultural Teaching—Plans for Race, Class, Gender, and Disability.* Upper Saddle River, NJ: Merrill.

———. 1999. *Making Choices for Multicultural Education: Five Approaches to Race, Class, and Gender.* Upper Saddle River, NJ: Merrill.

Wood, George. 1990. "Teaching for Democracy." *Educational Leadership* 48, no. 3: 32.

"Youth OUTreach." Available at LAMBDA GLBT Community Services Web site, http://www.lambda.org/.

Chapter Two

❧ Origins of Multicultural Education

In establishing a chronology of multicultural and diversity education for the United States, it is important to recognize the impossibility of "reading backwards" onto history our own historically idiosyncratic interest in a certain sort of multicultural society. It is difficult to overlay a template of multiculturalism onto a world that did not think in such "modern" terms. It is equally problematic to establish multiculturalism as a contemporary guide to understanding our own history because the notion itself must be held up for questioning—even as we read and write this, multiculturalism as a historically contingent term arose in the 1970s and 1980s, was implemented within education mostly within the 1980s and 1990s, and was then reexamined as a culturally valued term in the 1990s and into the current century.

THE DANGER OF REVISIONIST HISTORY

As Michael Olneck wrote in 1990,

> If pluralism is to have a meaning distinct from mere diversity, it must recognize, in some serious manner, the identities and claims of groups *as groups*. Multicultural education, instead, is largely constructed around the concept of "individual difference," advances an apolitical and fragmented model of culture, and presumes an attitudinal explanation for ethnic conflict. (Olneck 1990, 147)

Olneck has researched the ways in which contemporary approaches to multicultural education reproduce earlier educational reform movements of differing ideological and situational origins. For example, he describes the ways in which school practices of the 1970s and 1980s reflect a common heritage shared with the intercultural education and cultural integration efforts of the 1930s and 1940s. Interculturalists were ambiguous about cultural diversity in American life. They attributed ethnic, racial, and religious tensions to misconceptions about cultural differences, and sought to refute popular beliefs invoked to justify prejudice and discrimination. Multiculturalism, however, is clear on its view of pluralism and diversity. It replaces a restrained recognition of diverse characteristics with a celebration of differences and an endorsement of distinctive cultural identities. Even multiculturalism, however, is critiqued as reifying cultural categories and erasing the complexity of identity processes (see Chapter 5). That is, multiculturalism has tended to turn ideas into things that are then understood as facts, or truths, about how the world works.

Diversity education is often associated with emerging notions of "equality" in education. This term, too, is confusing to read back into history, for the meaning of equality is as contingent on context as its use in rhetorical arguments. Equality might refer to equality of opportunity, or to equality of outcomes; it may have something to do with equality of participation or equality of value. Multiculturalism as a reform movement has been described as shifting the meanings of equality away from an emphasis on hierarchy and belonging, toward highlighting inclusion and community. Nevertheless, while the accepted meanings of equality today have been broadened a bit to include an absence of bias in curricular materials and the (utopian) representation of equal status among racial and ethnic groups, the application and relevance of these meanings have mostly been narrowly constrained (Olneck 1993). Thus, although multiculturalism—especially as understood within the contexts of diversity education and critical multiculturalism—continues to offer potential for reordering our notions of political relationships and for redefining legitimacy of school subject content, it remains essentially untapped in its efforts to establish new symbolic meanings related to status and equality in many ways.

It is with the above comments in mind that this handbook offers the following discussion of the history and origins of multicultural and diversity education. Much of the debate on multicultural education is conducted about the term of "distributive equality." In this discourse, resources are equally distributed, or access to resources is maintained for "equal opportunity." Bilingual education, for example, is defended and critiqued on the basis of its capacity to raise test scores and grades and to reduce dropout rates. More innovative approaches such as Afrocentric education or Latino American immersion schools also claim they enhance achievement and retention in school. Yet other criteria of success would surely be relevant to an appraisal of bilingual or ethnic programs. The principle that the curriculum must be unbiased and must represent and include the roles and contributions of all groups is no longer controversial in most places; what this means, however, is still very controversial and becomes a focal point for conflict when the status of programs is under scrutiny. The principle that pedagogy should be responsive to diverse learning styles is widely accepted but generally poorly implemented; professional development toward such practices remains on a superficial introductory level, and serious efforts to transform teaching styles are often incompatible with forms of school organization and traditional expectations of classroom practice.

We begin with a brief overview of the origins of cultural awareness and diversity concerns related to U.S. education, focusing in particular on the historical trajectories of deculturalization, segregation, and integration. Our collection of stories continues with attention to the differing notions of education as Americanization. Our chronology of the late twentieth century highlights the role of the civil rights movement, the emergence of multiculturalism as a social and political force, and the "culture wars" toward the end of that century. Recent history focuses on the rise of globalization and the "creolization of culture" (the intermixing of cultures to form new cultures), the politics of identity, the increasing sophistication of diversity education efforts, and the emergence of postmodern critiques of multiculturalism.

DECULTURALIZATION, SEGREGATION, AND INTEGRATION

Lawrence Cremin (1980) begins his chapter on "outcasts" of the U.S. educational experience by referring to Frederick Grimke and Alexis de Tocqueville, political theorists of the nineteenth century who presupposed the United States as a society of free individuals who could express themselves openly on matters of public interest, and freely organize into associations of like-minded individuals. Likewise, early U.S. writers assumed citizens were prepared, able, and at liberty to state their opinions, acting on their preferences at the ballot box, in public office, and in the more general realm of civil and cultural affairs. Yet there were profound anomalies in this view of U.S. society, Cremin writes: although Grimke recognized that people are best educated to freedom by being given the experience of freedom, he drew back from the logic of that argument when it came to blacks and American Indians. He maintained that they belonged to races decidedly inferior to whites and hence would not profit from the experience, a perspective pervasive among his countrymen. Toqueville, as a detached observer of U.S. culture, described blacks and Indians as typically American but decidedly undemocratic. "These two unhappy races," he remarked, "have nothing in common, neither birth, nor features, nor language, nor habits. Their only resemblance lies in their misfortunes. Both of them occupy an equally inferior position in the country they inhabit; both suffer from tyranny; and if their wrongs are not the same, they originate from the same authors" (218–219). Enforced servitude, he continued, would deny civilization to the blacks, while enforced segregation would deny it to the freed blacks; a self-chosen "barbarous independence" would deny it to the Indians (219). In the absence of civilization, neither race could ever assimilate into the American community.

It is in these sorts of remarks that we can understand one facet of the origins of multicultural education. A view of civilization, assimilation, and racial coexistence was part and parcel of living the educational institutions of American life from colonial times through the nineteenth and twentieth centuries, and continues to the present. Joel Spring (1997) characterizes this history as the play among forces and efforts of deculturalization, segregation, and integration. Deculturalization refers to the stripping away of a people's culture and replacing it with a new culture. This indeed was the method used by the U.S. government after the conquest of Native Americans. In the nineteenth century, U.S. government leaders and educators rejected the concept of the United States as a multicultural society for a society unified around Protestant Anglo-American culture. In addition, government leaders believed that deculturalization was necessary in order to win the loyalty of conquered Native Americans to the U.S. government. As part of the deculturalization process, federal and state governments instituted programs of Americanization designed to replace native cultures with the dominant white culture of the United States.

Feelings of superiority were embedded in beliefs about the "manifest destiny" of the nation. Cremin disagrees with Spring, quoting a number of sources that suggest that colonial Americans did not even think that deculturalization was possible. "Educate him," the Connecticut Colonialization Society declared in 1828 of the emancipated African American, "and you have added little or nothing to his happiness—you have unfitted him for the society and sympathies of degraded kindred, and yet you have not procured for him and cannot procure for him any admission into the society and sympathy of white men" (242). Although Native Americans were in general deemed to some extent assimilable, outbursts of response to the proximity of mission schools and occasional intermarriages led to the closing of schools; the proclamation of the independent Cherokee Nation in 1827 strengthened views that destruction of native culture and removal to distant territory west of the Mississippi were the only options. Sociopolitical approaches to education were correlated to these beliefs.

Other subcommunities experienced related dynamics of differentiated education during the nineteenth century, but they did so differently. The Irish Catholic families of New York City during the 1850s and 1860s, crowded as they were into increasingly homogeneous immigrant neighborhoods, developed their own configurations of Irish households, Irish churches, Irish schools, Irish benevolent societies, and Irish newspapers. New York City in turn offered public schools, dozens of alternative churches and newspapers, a variety of social services conducted by benevolent organizations representing the missionary thrust of the evangelical united front, and a dazzling array of social and vocational apprenticeships, most of which were unavailable to the Irish. Much the same could be said about the German Lutherans who settled in Lancaster, Pennsylvania, the Norwegian and Swedish immigrants who settled on the farmlands of Wisconsin and Minnesota, the Mexican immigrants who settled in towns of Texas, and the Chinese and Japanese immigrants who settled in the cities of California and Washington. Given the prevalence of discordant education, the crucial variable, writes Cremin, was race. The assumption of the dominant white community with respect to the Irish Catholics, the German Lutherans, and the Norwegian and Swedish Reformed was that they needed to be and could be Americanized—a concept that was widely used to imply some combination of learning English, understanding the Constitution, living productively within the law according to middle-class standards, and accepting the values of a nondenominational Protestant milieu. Looked at another way, education was an institution of racism that characterized races and classified them as assimilable or not, and feared practices such as intergroup marriage and "passing," which were regarded as "confusion" on the part of the nondominant members as to their "place" in society.

Important to understand is that not all those thought of as "foreign" were "immigrants." The evolution of discriminatory attitudes and practices toward Mexican Americans occurred in two stages. According to Spring (1997), "the first stage involved the treatment of the Mexicans who remained after conquest. The second stage occurred in the late nineteenth and early twentieth centuries, when U.S. farmers encouraged the immigration of farm laborers from Mexico, and political and economic conditions in Mexico caused many Mexicans to seek residence in the United States" (78). This latter wave of immigration has left many to interpret the plight of Mexican Americans as another example of immigration-related practices, when in fact the history has much to do with the relationship of a conquered people to its conqueror. As with Native Americans and Puerto Ricans, deculturalization included a mandate for English in the schools, U.S. patriotic curricula, and segregation in schooling. Conflicting attitudes surfaced. On the one hand, farmers did not want Mexican children to go to school because school attendance meant that they were not available for farm work. Indeed Guadalupe San Miguel (1987) writes that one of the most discriminatory acts against children of Mexicans was the nonenforcement of compulsory school laws in the twentieth century. On the other hand, many public officials wanted Mexican children in school so that they could be "Americanized." At the same time, many Mexican families were reluctant to send their children to school because of the loss of the children's contribution to the family income. In addition to outright racism toward Mexican Americans, school segregation was justified by the same argument used to justify isolating southeastern Indians in Indian Territory: segregation would provide the opportunity to Americanize the child in a controlled linguistic and cultural environment, and to train the students for occupations considered open to and appropriate for them.

The civil rights movement of the 1960s and 1970s was a response to culture wars initiated by English colonists when they invaded Native American lands in North America. From the time of the invasion through the twentieth century, many people tried, and continue to try, to maintain Protestant Anglo-American culture as the dominant culture of the United States. William Bennett, former secretary of education and an outspoken voice on contemporary education reform, criticized much of the work in multicultural curriculum development in the 1980s. In response to professionals who identified a "loss of voice" and "deepening crisis" in backlashes to multiculturalism (Apple 1990, 527), Bennett characterized the multicultural movement in the following terms: "we simply stopped doing the right things [and] allowed an assault on intellectual and moral standards." This assault had, in Bennett's opinion, led schools away from "the principles of our tradition" (Bennett 1988, 10).

The great civil rights movement, composed of minority groups who protested the domination of Protestant Anglo-American culture (supported by sympathetic members of white culture who recognized its inherent oppression), demanded recognition and restoration of their own cultures. Many activists rejected the idea of a single dominating culture and imagined a pluralistic society. In the area of education, this meant giving recognition to these many cultures in the schools. But it also meant the end of segregation and racism in educational practices. Leading the way was the National Association for the Advancement of Colored People (NAACP), which "fought the continuation of segregation in schools and public facilities, and the lack of opportunity to participate in the American economic system. In addition, they demanded that African American culture be part of the school curriculum" (Spring 1997, 93).

The actions of African Americans contributed to the militancy of other groups in demanding equality of educational opportunity and recognition of their cultures in public schools. Native Americans campaigned for self-determination and cultural recognition. Mexican Americans continued their struggles against segregation and sought preservation of Mexican culture and the Spanish language in the schools. By the 1960s Puerto Ricans joined Mexican Americans in supporting bilingual education. Also, the "civil rights movement opened the door to demands that the public schools reflect minority cultures. African Americans, Native Americans, Mexican Americans, Asian Americans, [and Puerto Ricans] demanded that their unique cultures be given a place in the school curriculum" (Spring 1997, 93). And many whites who grew up in the latter part of the twentieth century also feel that all citizens of their country should be represented and respected by the school curriculum.

CHRONOLOGY

1780s—Noah Webster's Blue-backed Speller

Commonly referred to as the "Schoolmaster of America," Webster was passionately committed to a United States free of decadent European influence and with strong, uniquely American citizenship and institutions. His system of instruction in reading and writing was aimed at developing patriotic Americans and creating a unified national spirit. The speller instilled respect for hard work and property rights. By 1875, 75 million copies of Webster's blue-backed speller had been sold. Its popularity attests to its match with what people already thought children should learn. Once the speller became the "standard" text, it set a curriculum pattern—of infusing political and moral content into teaching basic skills. Webster's speller was echoed in the 1990s by then-Secretary of Education William Bennett, who decried what he saw as the erosion of explicit moral content in the schools. He published his own best-seller, *The Book of Virtues,* which led to a series of videotapes for children that used classic stories and fairy tales as the vehicle for teaching morals to children.

1790—Naturalization Act

This law denied U.S. citizenship to immigrants from Africa and Asia, and to Native Americans. Race was primarily defined by skin color. During its more than 150 years of existence, this law was used by members of federal and state governments to keep the population primarily white. Asian Americans were the largest immigrant group affected by the Naturalization Act, which allowed only whites to become citizens. The law was used to deny Asian immigrants the right to own property.

Early-Nineteenth-Century Education

African American schools in Boston were successful. Decisions by whites to take over the schools led to decreased performance and increased disillusionment with the schools. Native American–run schools produced almost 100 percent literacy rates, a level of English higher in western Oklahoma Cherokees than in the white populations of either Texas or Arkansas. With the institution of white-run boarding schools, the literacy rate plummeted to less than 10 percent. After much legal contention, the California school code provided for segregated Chinese schools in 1885.

German schools in the Midwest successfully maintained language and cultural traditions. Swedish culture schools included traditional crafts and textile work as a central component of the curriculum.

The 1830s and 1840s

In mid-century a movement began for "common schools" (schools in which all shared a common interest) that would provide the same curriculum to all. Working-class people, immigrants, and those outside the dominant culture who lacked the resources for their own private schools saw the common school as a path to the American dream. People of greater wealth and status saw their own well-being enhanced by common schools, even if their children did not attend them. Everyone would benefit, they reasoned, if schools could turn out productive workers and good citizens.

> Prior to the 1900s, bilingual and non-English educational programs
> in German, French, Italian, and Spanish existed throughout the
> United States. (In 1900 more than 600,000 elementary school stu-
> dents—about 4 percent of the primary school population—received
> instruction at least partly in German.) Such programs declined in
> use during the early 1900s, however, when waves of anti-immigrant
> feeling led to restrictions on the use of languages other than English
> in classrooms. (http://student.csumb.edu/students_s-z/salcido
> christi/world/salcido_ERD/salcido_assess.htm)

Early-Twentieth-Century Efforts toward Pluralism and Intercultural Education

Jane Addams founded Hull House in Chicago in 1899, and Hull House became the best known of the big city settlement houses that helped immigrants adjust to American life. Hull House was the center of a rich intellectual and cultural community out of which grew a number of ideas for cultural pluralism in the school curriculum. Addams, John Dewey, and others argued that although everyone should learn the common culture—English, U.S. history, and the U.S. political system—immigrants should also retain their home cultures. Culturalists pressed for a curriculum that included handicrafts and occupations, cultural traditions, folk songs and folklore, and the stories of nonwhite and immigrant students.

Booker T. Washington had established Tuskegee University in 1881 with such values in mind, but also placated many scared whites by accomplishing his work in a segregated setting. W. E. B. DuBois passionately called for engaging students with the ideas and "truths" of diverse people, particularly those not usually heard in definitions of what is and dreams of what might be. Mordecai Kaplan established a definition of hyphenated Americanism for Jewish Americans, which was adaptable to other cultural subgroups. He also created a system of pluralist Jewish identity, making it possible for U.S. Jews to accept differences within their subgroup identity. This, too, was adaptable to other cultural groups, so that racial, ethnic, religious, and other identities could be understood as multiple and conflicting even as people began to celebrate the possibilities for recognition by the school curriculum and the dominant culture.

Intercultural and International Education

Before, during, and after World War I, intercultural education and international education became popular ideas among educators and social reformers. Concerned about the dangers of international conflict, many sought ways for people to learn about other cultures in the hopes of eliminating conflicts both internationally (thus international education) and domestically (intercultural education) as the diversity of the population increased, especially in urban areas.

The 1928 Merriam Report

This U.S. government–commissioned report declared a need to change the deculturalization approach to Indian education. In the past, educators had proceeded largely on the theory that it was necessary to remove the Indian child as far as possible from his or her home environment. The Merriam Report completely reversed this philosophy, stating that modern education and social work emphasized the value of an upbringing in the natural setting of home and family. This notion of family involvement as central to educational efforts was to reemerge in the late twentieth century as a critical tenet of multicultural school reform.

1954—Brown v. Board of Education

This landmark U.S. Supreme Court decision called for an end to segregation in public schools. The Court decreed, "In the field of public education the doctrine of 'separate but equal' has no place. Separate educational facilities are inherently unequal."

The Civil Rights Movement and Subsequent Social Movements

The evolution of the mass media in the 1950s was an important factor in the civil rights movement because it became possible to turn local problems into national issues. It was possible to force many people in the United States to confront racism and the legacy of oppression arising from slavery. Spring writes, "Concern over America's international image grew as pictures of racial injustice flashed around the world, and the president's public image was often threatened when examples of racial injustice were shown to millions of television viewers and the question was asked, What is our president doing about this situation?" (96). The most dramatic technique used by civil rights groups was nonviolent confrontation, a strategy introduced by the Christian student movement of the 1930s and promoted by Martin Luther King, Jr. The Congress on Racial Equality (CORE) and other organizations were committed to Mahatma Gandhi's technique of *satyagraha* (nonviolent direct action) in solving racial and industrial problems. As civil rights demonstrations increased in intensity, national leaders began to work for federal legislation, leading eventually to the Civil Rights Act of 1964. Title VI, the most important section for education, established the precedent for using the disbursement of government money as a means of controlling educational policies. It required withholding of federal funds from institutions that did not comply with its mandates that no person, on the basis of race, color, or national origin, could be excluded from or denied the benefits of any program receiving federal financial assistance. All federal agencies were required to establish guidelines to implement this policy. Other social movements, such as the women's movement, the gay rights movement, and the efforts to claim rights of people with disabilities, were modeled upon the successes and failures of the civil rights movement.

1965—Immigration Act

This congressional act removed the quota system and the restrictions of the 1924 immigration act. The new wave of immigration to the United States occurred at the same time that Native Americans, Mexican Americans, Puerto Ricans, and African Americans were demanding a place for their cultures in the public school curriculum. As a result of these demands and the problems posed in educating a new wave of immigrants, educators began talking about teaching a variety of cultures (multiculturalism).

1960s and 1970s—Afrocentric and Latinocentric Curriculum Movements

Afrocentric and Latinocentric schools become visible as alternatives to traditional education. In the 1960s, a resurgence of interest in bilingual education accompanied the arrival in Florida of Spanish-speaking refugees from Cuba.

> During the 1960s, Mexican Americans began to demonstrate for the use of Spanish in schools and the teaching of Mexican-American history and culture. In 1968 Mexican American students boycotted four East Los Angeles high schools, demanding bilingual programs, courses in Mexican-American history and culture, and the serving of Mexican food in the school cafeterias; [they also] demanded the hiring of more Spanish-speaking teachers. . . . The school boycotts in Los Angeles attracted the attention of the newly formed La Raza Unida, which took a militant stand on the protection of the rights of Mexican Americans. (Spring 1997, 107)

Politicians responded to Mexican American and Puerto Rican demands for the presentation of Spanish in the schools. Native American communities also supported bilingual education. Senator Ralph Yarborough of Texas, concerned about his ability to win the 1970 election, decided that Hispanic support was crucial to his coalition and began hearings with representatives of the Mexican American and Puerto Rican communities; the hearings concluded in East Harlem and led to the passage of the Bilingual Education Act in 1968.

Bilingual education in some contexts led to "bicultural education" curricula, which were designed to enable students to become bi-cultural: understanding the expectations and interaction styles of one's own culture and the dominant culture at the same time. Extensions of this concept fed into some "multicultural" curricula.

1974—Lau v. Nichols

The U.S. Supreme Court decision in *Lau* v. *Nichols* mandated language education for students lacking proficiency in English. The decision stated that providing instruction only in English does not constitute equal treatment for such students. In order to learn, students must have the ability to engage in meaningful discourse with other students and teachers. Therefore, requiring mastery of basic English skills prior to participating in the educational process unfairly handicaps limited English-proficiency (LEP) students. Many people interpreted this decision as reversing the important thrust of *Brown v. Board of Education,* because this new decision seemed to say that separate educational programs are required for equity.

Although federal law requires schools to help LEP students understand classroom instruction, it does not specify the techniques schools may use to meet this mandate. Schools generally offer two basic kinds of educational programs to meet the needs of LEP students: bilingual education and English as a Second Language (ESL). Schools with ESL programs provide instruction by teachers trained to teach students whose native language is not English. ESL teachers conduct instruction in English in a way that is understandable for nonnative English speakers. Schools often provide ESL programs when they have too few students who share the same native language to offer bilingual instruction. Some schools offer both ESL and bilingual educational programs. In 1994, 76 percent of public schools in the United States with LEP student enrollments provided ESL programs and 36 percent had bilingual education programs.

1975—Individuals with Disabilities Education Act; Education of All Handicapped Children Act

Despite the civil rights movement heightening awareness of discrimination, the federal Civil Rights Act of 1964 applied only to people who were discriminated against on the basis of race, color, sex, religion, or national origin. At that time, discrimination against people with disabilities remained legally acceptable. The Rehabilitation Act of 1973 protected employment rights for people with disabilities. However, that act applied only to businesses that received federal financial assistance. The vast majority of private employers and businesses, as well as most local governments, were not required to comply. The limited applicability of the act, along with inconsistent implementation of its requirements, spurred people with disabilities to seek greater legal protection of their civil rights. The 1975 Individuals with Disabilities Education Act guaranteed a public education to children with a broad range of disabilities. However, none of the laws passed during this time dealt with the problem of discrimination against people with disabilities in the critical areas of employment, access to governmental services, and public accommodations. Passage by Congress of the Education of All Handicapped Children Act of 1975 extended the right of equal educational opportunity to children with disabilities.

1980s—Culture Wars

The cultural ambivalence of U.S. society resurfaced with calls to preserve the principles and standards upon which essential morals are maintained. Allan Bloom, in *The Closing of the American Mind,* wrote that "culture means a war against chaos *and* a war against other cultures." People argued that without clear sets of principles and standards, students would continue a decades-long collapse into a relativism that undermines the moral grounding of the nation. E. D. Hirsch published *Cultural Literacy,* in which he proposed two forms of multiculturalism: First is the ethical, progressive, cosmopolitan form he advocated, which considered ethnicity an accident of history, having little to do with defining one's identity and cultural essence. This form of multiculturalism encourages sympathy for other cultures and respect for one's own, but stresses competence in the current system of language and allusion that is dominant in the nation's economic and intellectual discourse. Second, Hirsch's "retrogressive and ethnocentric" form of multiculturalism sets groups against each other, and in his mind hinders the educational excellence and fairness it was mistakenly conceived to enhance. Adherents of this notion claimed that children may learn a great deal about, for example, their African and African American past, but that this learning is at the expense of learning to read, write, solve mathematical problems effectively, and understand natural science. Others argued that it is absurd to read multiculturalism as victimizing minority children by preventing them from participating in the mainstream culture; the disastrous failures of earlier attempts at teaching traditional subject matter in traditional ways and of integrated and thematic curricula called, in their mind, for something new.

1990s—Teaching the "Codes of Power"

Gloria Ladson-Billings published *The Dreamkeepers,* about outstanding teachers of African American children. Using the language of successful teachers, she conveyed recent sociological theory and research about how both the content and the structures of schooling connect with social class and racial stratification. Just as dollars have purchasing power, certain cultural knowledge, tastes, and habits have exchange values that sociologists call *cultural capital.* In schools, jobs, and social interactions generally, certain habits and knowledge "buy" acceptance or favored treatment. Lisa Delpit framed schools' attempts to respond to issues raised by multiculturalism as well-intentioned liberalism run amok. In *Other People's Children,* she decried the plight of many students who are taught as the "culturally different." This book also asked questions about how children gain access to the knowledge and skills that they will need to participate fully in the culture, underscoring the need for children to understand that they are learning a particular code of power and not simply the "right" or "best" culture and language. Sonia Nieto's *Affirming Diversity* included case studies of twelve diverse students and how schooling intersected with their lives, making another strong case for a sociopolitical approach to multicultural education.

According to Jeannie Oakes and Martin Lipton, sociocultural pedagogy *expects* difference. This presumes that there is no central "norm" by which others are compared and judged. Such a position does not mean that we are "color-blind," ignoring differences or pretending that differences are not important. Nor does it mean remaining silent in the face of hurtful or immoral behavior. It means celebrating differences in multidimensional classrooms. In a community of diverse learners, everybody is smart, and differences are the source of rich learning interactions. Teachers make each student's particular competence visible to scaffold one another's learning, and to combine their different knowledge and experiences into the learning community's experiences.

1990—National Association for Multicultural Education (NAME)

NAME was founded to bring together educators who have an interest in multicultural education. Its quarterly magazine, *Multicultural Education,* features sections with promising practices and resources for teachers. The organization's annual conference provides an opportunity for intensive discussion and learning.

Professional associations in the various traditional disciplines of U.S. education established standards for the teaching and assessment of their subject areas, including aspects of multicultural education; state curricula frameworks and high-stakes testing both institutionalized many of these standards by incorporating them into policies, and also created conflicts with multicultural practices by setting them in opposition to what the public perceived as "testable."

1990—Americans with Disabilities Act; Individuals with Disabilities Education Act

The Americans with Disabilities Act (ADA) was first introduced in Congress in mid-1988, but Congress did not adopt the law during that session. The bill was strongly opposed by many corporate interests, who feared compliance would be costly. Others argued that the legislation was not needed or was unenforceable. When the bill was reintroduced in the following congressional session, both the Senate and the House of Representatives passed it by overwhelming majorities. The turnaround was due to support by a vast coalition of organizations representing people with disabilities. These organizations launched an intensive campaign to change legislators' votes, culminating in March 1990 with a massive demonstration at the Capitol in Washington, D.C. President George Bush signed the act into law on July 26, 1990.

Unlike earlier laws that were much more limited in scope, the ADA forbids unequal treatment of people with disabilities in a broad variety of circumstances. To obtain the protections provided by the ADA, a person must either have a physical or mental impairment that substantially limits one or more major life activities, have a record of such an impairment, or be regarded as having such an impairment. Major life activities include walking, speaking, breathing, seeing, hearing, learning, working, caring for oneself, and performing tasks that involve use of the hands. Several federal government agencies, such as the Equal Employment Opportunity Commission (EEOC), the Department of Justice (DOJ), the Department of Transportation (DOT), and the Federal Communications Commission (FCC), enforce different provisions of the ADA.

The Individuals with Disabilities Education Act (IDEA) reenacted the themes and provisions of the similar acts of the 1970s, and has undergone numerous amendments. IDEA ensures that all children, even those with severe disabilities, have the opportunity to receive a free and appropriate public education in the least restrictive environment. The IDEA, together with the ADA, reflected a growing awareness among legislators and educators that separating children with disabilities from children without disabilities constitutes unequal education.

1990s—White Studies

White identity development became an area of research predominantly by African American psychologists who included race as a dimension of identity and whose theoretical construction of white identity originated in their study of black racial identity. The aptness of this approach to the study of race and the impact of teachers' and students' race on the possibilities for multicultural education were quickly recognized, and white studies became a prominent feature of teacher preparation and diversity education. Because teachers and prospective teachers are overwhelmingly white, teacher educators and those working in professional development assumed that race consciousness was an essential predisposition to eradicating racist policies and practices in schooling. Critics saw white studies as perpetuating a white-centered view of educational practices.

1995–1998—Pedagogy and Theater of the Oppressed Conference

Liberatory practitioners including educators, critical pedagogists, activist artists, and community activists formed an annual conference and a networking community to promote work applying the ideas of Paulo Freire and Augusto Boal, incorporating critical pedagogy and theater. In Theater of the Oppressed performances, audience members and performers interact with each other, and audience members are encouraged to join the performance. Through this participation, audience members become empowered not only to imagine change but to actually practice that change and to reflect collectively on their suggestions. They are empowered to generate social action. Theater becomes a form of experiential learning and a practical vehicle for grassroots activism.

1995—Vivian Gussin Paley

With her publication of *Kwanzaa and Me* (1995), Vivian Gussin Paley, a prolific writer and kindergarten teacher, revisits her earlier work in *White Teacher* (1979). Still believing in her efforts to promote a pluralist curriculum, she includes the voice of a previous student who loved her but now believes an African American school would have been a better place to learn. In *The Girl with the Brown Crayon* (1997) and *The Kindness of Children* (2000), she attempts to uphold multicultural educational practices as based in sound universal moral virtues, continuing the themes of her earlier work and building on *You Can't Say You Can't Play* (1992).

1990s—Education for a Global and Technological Society

The rise of the Internet, along with growth in technology and globalization, led many to conclude that young people more than ever need to understand global cultures, and to interact with diverse people across the globe with and without technology. Recalling earlier confusions between international, intercultural, and multicultural education, late-twentieth-century practices demonstrated how far they were removed from the sophisticated conceptual understanding that had emerged in the previous two decades. One common response to the problems of language proficiency raised by globalization is the establishment of dual-language programs, in which students alternate days of instruction in English and another language, commonly Spanish, Chinese, or French. Large sums of money are spent in making schools and classrooms Internet-accessible; these funding programs are often justified in terms of technology for globalization as well as important preparation for a technology-rich job market. In general, these technological programs are outdated by the time they are completed.

1998–1999 Supreme Court Decisions

The Supreme Court has issued a number of rulings that clarify who is considered disabled under the ADA and what constitutes discrimination under ADA. In a 1998 decision in *Bragdon v. Abbott*, the Court ruled that people infected with human immunodeficiency virus (HIV) qualify as disabled under the ADA. HIV is the virus that causes acquired immunodeficiency syndrome (AIDS). Even though many people with HIV show no symptoms, the Court ruled that having HIV substantially limits reproduction, which it considered a major life activity. Also in 1998 the Court ruled in *Pennsylvania Department of Corrections v. Yeskey* that state prisons must comply with the provisions of the ADA and make reasonable accommodations for people with disabilities.

In a series of rulings issued in 1999, the Court limited who can be considered disabled under the ADA. In *Sutton* v. *United Air Lines, Inc.*, *Murphy v. United Parcel Service, Inc.*, and *Albertsons, Inc. v. Kirkingburg*, the Court found that people whose impairments are correctable are not considered disabled under the ADA. Thus, the ADA does not protect from discrimination people with vision problems that can be corrected by eyeglasses, nor does the law apply to people with medical conditions such as diabetes or high blood pressure that can be controlled by medication. The Court also ruled that companies may define some physical standards that workers must meet to hold certain jobs. The decisions generally pleased employers because the narrower definition of disability removed the possibility that they would have to make expensive accommodations for huge numbers of employees. Advocates for people with disabilities said the Court had undercut the law.

REFERENCES AND FURTHER READING

Apple, Michael. 1990. "Is There a Curriculum Voice to Reclaim?" *Phi Delta Kappan* 71, no. 7: 526–530.

Bennett, William J. 1988. *Our Children and Our Country.* New York: Simon and Schuster.

Bloom, Allan. 1988. *The Closing of the American Mind: How Higher Education Failed Democracy and Impoverished the Souls of Today's Students.* New York: Touchstone Books.

Cremin, Lawrence. 1980. *American Education: The National Experience, 1783–1876.* New York: Harper.

Delpit, Lisa. 1995. *Other People's Children: Cultural Conflict in the Classroom.* New York: The New Press.

Hirsch, E. D. 1998. *Cultural Literacy: What Every American Needs to Know.* New York: Vintage Books.

Ladson-Billings, Gloria. 1994. *The Dreamkeepers: Successful Teachers of African American Children.* San Francisco: Jossey-Bass.

Nieto, Sonia. 1996. *Affirming Diversity: Sociopolitical Context of Multicultural Education.* New York: Longman.

Oakes, Jeannie, and Martin Lipton. 1999. *Teaching to Change the World.* Boston: McGraw-Hill.

Olneck, Michael. 1990. "The Recurring Dream: Symbolism and Ideology in Intercultural and Multicultural Education." *American Journal of Education* (February): 147–174.

———. 1993. "Terms of Inclusion: Has Multiculturalism Redefined Equality in American Education?" *American Journal of Education* 101 (May): 234–260.

Paley, Vivian Gussin. 1979. *White Teacher.* Cambridge, MA: Harvard University Press.

———. 1992. *You Can't Say You Can't Play.* Cambridge, MA: Harvard University Press.

———. 1995. *Kwanzaa and Me.* Cambridge, MA: Harvard University Press.

———. 1997. *The Girl with the Brown Crayon.* Cambridge, MA: Harvard University Press.

———. 2000. *The Kindness of Children.* Cambridge, MA: Harvard University Press.

San Miguel, Guadalupe. 1987. *Let All of Them Take Heed: Mexican Americans and the Campaign for Educational Equality in Texas, 1910–1981.* Austin: University of Texas Press.

Spring, Joel. 1997. *Deculturalization and the Struggle for Equality: A Brief History of the Education of Dominated Cultures in the United States.* New York: McGraw-Hill.

Chapter Three

ᵒ⬥ Curricular Approaches

WHY MULTICULTURAL EDUCATION?

In the early twenty-first century, there remain several arguments for diversity education, including those highlighting issues of equity and those growing out of the frustrations of families, teachers, administrators, and members of the community. This chapter will explore curricular responses to these issues and frustrations. Three areas of educational practice that pose the most direct challenge to multicultural and diversity education are assessment, classroom management, and grouping practices. In each of these areas, traditional practices and assumptions about appropriate school structure undermine changes that must occur for pluralistic and democratic education to exist.

Equity Issues

An increasingly pluralist society demands a pluralist curriculum. Indicators of equality of opportunity and equality of educational outcomes (see Chapter 1) call for responses to the diverse school population in order to achieve both types of equity. In assessment practices, this means establishing vehicles for *all* students to demonstrate what they have learned and what they can do, including enabling students to be diverse in the ways in which they demonstrate their accomplishments. In the classroom and school community, multicultural and diversity education demand that all participants respect one another and work together to solve common problems; the accent is on supporting the academic development of all members of the classroom, and the responsibility of each participant in making the community a success. Grouping practices raise serious questions for multiculturalists, because these practices respond to differences by attempting to carefully respond to the needs of particular groups, and at the same time they create inequities and categories of difference that work against diversity goals of including everyone in the community.

Teachers' Frustrations

Considering how elaborately intertwined racial and other stereotypes are with perceptions of academic ability, it is almost futile for teachers to try to increase acceptance of diversity in their classrooms unless they actively work to change perceptions about who is able. Most teachers value and want to be sensitive to students' differences. But traditional classroom organization and practices can defy these values until even the most well-intentioned teachers become partners in establishing their students' low levels of confidence and low status. Multi-ability lessons sound good in theory but there are few models of such lessons for teachers to emulate, and even when teachers are successful with new practices, they receive complaints that their classrooms do not look like "school."

Teachers need to be confident that they can indeed teach all students successfully. But this self-efficacy is undermined by lockstep curricula, fixed time limits, and customary grouping practices. These traditional practices reinforce narrow conceptions of successful achievement and limit who can succeed. Lessons that are based on sociocultural theories promote a cycle of students' participation and achievement that is energized by and promotes teachers' confidence as well as the students' confidence. However, when they are asked to make sure that their students perform well on standardized high-stakes exams, teachers find little room for authentic assessment of what their students understand.

Students' Frustrations

Most teachers, striving for quiet and efficient classrooms, organize their instruction to control or minimize activity and social interactions. Teachers talk to the whole class at once, they walk around the room giving individual help, they call on students to read aloud to the class, answer questions, or write on the board. Students quickly learn to identify the behaviors that school adults want from them. Children who can, or who decide they can, learn to listen for the answers that please adults, and they become skilled at repeating them even when they have not learned the underlying concepts. Occasionally, classroom activities make it necessary or appropriate for students to talk and work together—perhaps in cooperative learning groups. But many teachers believe and demonstrate to their students that the most important school time is the classwork and evaluation that have students compete against one another or work alone. After a short time in school, students decide that the "real" learning is what they do by themselves.

Families' and Communities' Frustrations

For many students, performing well for adults in the school means talking differently and thinking differently from family, friends, and community. In some communities there is evidence of the delayed gratification of rewards for good school performance. Performing well does not necessarily lead to such rewards for *all* members of a community, however. It is not clear that the deculturalization demanded by performing well is worth the effort. New teaching practices suggest to parents and families that the school does not believe their children can handle the "real" school they expect, even if these new practices are well-grounded in research and learning theory. At the same time, many of these new practices are tried out successfully in more affluent and suburban schools, leading to a perpetual cycle of cutting-edge schooling in the suburban, affluent communities, and old-fashioned and outmoded practices in urban and low-income communities. Special programs for low-performing schools identify such schools as "problems," creating a blame-the-victim mentality that causes insurmountable frustrations.

Administrators' Frustrations

Administrators seek multicultural and diversity education for a variety of purposes. They may hope that a more relevant curriculum for the students will lead to more engaged learning that can translate into higher test scores. They may be hoping that a better understanding and empathy will lead to improved intergroup relations among the students and staff of their school. They may simply be under pressure to respond to educational trends that call for multicultural education when they themselves see more immediate needs based on their local concerns. In general, however, the implementation of successful diversity practices requires extensive staff support and professional development. Often these practices assume a more democratic organizational structure than currently exists. Typically, curricular changes cannot be successful unless substantial adjustments to presumed organization of time and space are made. Facilitating genuine community involvement requires reskilling away from the controlled management of family and community members. Balancing such changes with the concerns and demands of community members and directives from the school board or superintendent's office can lead to numerous conflicts. More fundamentally, administrators have as little awareness of what educational alternatives might look like as the teachers in their schools, and far less time to devote to reorienting their perspectives. Implementation of multicultural and diversity practices requires a reconsideration of basic philosophical premises having to do with what knowledge is, whether human beings are inherently good or calculating, the role of power in society, and so on.

ASSESSMENT FOR MULTICULTURAL EDUCATION

It seems like everybody loves tests. Tests can be used to compare students' performance against a standard of particular knowledge, to compare students' performance to the performance of other students, and to compare students' performance on simulated tasks with the performance of someone already accomplished at the same task. Tests claim objectivity because they accept a set of practices, rules, and standards with which many people are familiar. They also sort for future opportunities by "tracking" students by their perceived abilities, although claiming to be fair and accurate in their measurements. But in the process of testing and using tests to compare and sort, educational institutions bypass concerns about the basic premises of tests, which are based on the assumption of a test-giver, and someone or some group of people empowered by the license to judge others; the test-giver gives the test to the test-taker, a person without power submitting to judgment. Traditional tests support traditional transmission models of learning and traditional behavioral expectations of students and teachers. But multicultural and diversity education questions the relevance of the knowledge to be tested, the power associated with testing, the fairness of the tests, the pedagogies required to prepare students for the tests, and the type of community relations possible when testing is central to that community.

Learning that proceeds from sociocultural and social justice perspectives is not compatible with the unbalanced and coercive relationships that traditional testing fosters. Ideally, a sociocultural vision of assessment is seamlessly integrated with the students' learning. This often means that the assessment and the scaffolding by which the teacher and student co-construct the student's new knowledge are indistinguishable. One way around traditional assessment problems is to create a parallel set of assessments: In this model, within the classroom and school community, authentic assessments are clearly valued and supported. At the same time, students study in preparation for standardized tests and discuss the very power relations and problems associated with these tests. In recognizing and responding to the inequities associated with the tests, students and teachers establish a form of social action curriculum. Multicultural educators sometimes refuse altogether to be implicated in the perpetuation of antidemocratic practices such as high-stakes testing. They may organize to protest such testing or boycott the administration of these tests. But no school is perfect. Such political action may undermine larger multicultural goals if the political work results in a loss of one's job. Because of this, many educators decide they can live with themselves if they choose the compromise route of parallel assessment. Still others believe the compromisers are deluding themselves as they perpetuate discrimination and the overemphasis on standards-based evaluation.

Assessment should be contrasted with evaluation. Most assessment done in schools today confuses assessment with evaluation. Evaluation could be taken to mean judging the quality of a student's performance. Assessment, on the other hand, is the collection of information with which educators can reflect on their practice and make decisions about future plans. Multicultural and diversity issues demand that assessment take diversity into account, searching for a variety of ways to enable students and teachers to understand how things are going in the classroom or school. Diversity education also requires that assessment be "authentic," or meaningful in real-world contexts closely entwined with instruction. Diversity educators encourage assessment to be interactive, with students and teachers participating collectively in the assessment processes.

CLASSROOM MANAGEMENT

Classroom management, discipline, and control dominate the worries of most teachers. They are responding to a never-ending stream of possible behavior situations that occur in classrooms. Many teachers' reputations rest on their ability to "control" classrooms. Partly, this emphasis on management is consistent with the historical continuity in education that expects schools to inculcate morals and discipline in addition to intellectual prowess. Traditions in education have made schools into places where academic learning is no more important than training children in proper behavior and in socializing children to act in conformity with social norms. This is part of the deculturalization process that has been a strong part of immigrant education as well. Schools have been modeled as efficient factories, in which students are trained to become dutiful workers and managers produce high-quality work. A science of education sets up some students as having "problem" behaviors that must be diagnosed and treated with prescriptions to eliminate social sickness (for example, the emphasis on Ritalin to control classroom-disruptive attention deficit disorder and hyperactivity in children). Behavior management that matches offenses with consequences is a form of such "medication."

Increasingly diverse student and staff populations bring with them controversies and disagreement about what constitutes "correct" behavior. And curricula that do not engage students in diverse ways lead to bored and disenchanted students who seek alleviation from the monotonous routines of school. Often students have not been part of establishing meaningful understanding of why certain behaviors are expected; in many cases students are not capable of meeting the expectations for physical, emotional, or other reasons. In socially just classrooms, there is a commitment to cultural relevance as a value, and constant attention to welcoming difference. Teachers are obligated to understand cultural ways of interacting, are responsive to cultural styles, are attentive to gender differences that appear in their classrooms, and strive to include every single member of the classroom community in the decision-making process about how that community works together. Students are recognized for the strengths they bring to the community and are accepted as "apprentices in democracy." Teachers in democratic classrooms also accept that it is not an easy task. It is a constant struggle to facilitate group dynamics. Things are always going wrong, but these are not problems: they are opportunities to work together as a community to understand what happened and why, to learn more about diversity, disagreement, and power, and to appreciate the experiences of each individual in the classroom.

GROUPING PRACTICES

A big challenge to diversity education is the way in which we group and organize students. This is a hard topic to understand because it seems so intelligent to identify the needs of students according to categories, and to respond to their needs with particularized instruction. The fact that there has been overwhelming research evidence that consistently demonstrates the harmful effects of most grouping practices has not helped us to eliminate these practices. One reason is the high value given to high-stakes testing. Indeed, studies do show that grouping students by perceived ability will in the short term help a school to raise the tests scores on a specific test if the students are then trained within their groups for the particular test. But research more clearly demonstrates higher-group advantages and lower-group disadvantages. Research also consistently shows advantages for *all* students in mixed-ability groups when meaningful instructional practices are employed.

Another reason it is difficult to understand the effects of grouping is that advanced placement programs and other accelerated or enrichment programs potentially conflict in their aims and their effects on the school community. Often these programs are employed to demonstrate that a wide variety of students are actually capable of serious academic work. If a school can put together a large number of diverse students to participate in such programs, people who believe in grouping (and especially grouping for challenging tests) will interpret this as a major accomplishment for the school and its students. However, the destructive forces set in motion by the existence of these programs, the separation of students as "in" or "out" of the programs, and the effect of these programs on the complicated scheduling requirements imposed by the creation of multiple grouping for some parts of the curriculum mostly damages the learning community irreparably. Special remedial programs are comparable in their effects. Often, *all* students would benefit from a special program, but only a few students have the opportunity.

CURRICULAR APPROACHES

Curriculum change is a starting place for many schools in making changes for multicultural and diversity education. Curriculum here has anything to do with content and delivery of instruction, the experience of learning and teaching, and the structure of the experience by cultural assumption, institutional policies, and utilization of the school and community resources. It is helpful to begin thinking "multiculturally" from the beginning of plans for curricular innovation. This means recognizing the need for diverse participation in planning and implementation. Diversity by any category not considered will lead to problems later on: if parents are excluded from decision making at early stages, parent resentment will foment and undermine later plans; if particular subgroups of parents are not included, then these subgroups will be bitter, disappointed, or alienated later on. It is up to facilitators of planning groups to research and understand the potential interests of any possible faction of teachers, families, staff, and other members of the school community, for the same reasons. Just as students and families may be affronted by the curriculum if they are expected to contribute the expert knowledge themselves, or are unable to adequately communicate pertinent information and contexts about a culture, participants in planning groups need to experience the safety and support that enables them to be themselves and not token representatives of a particular subgroup. Participants in curriculum transformation need to have already been exposed to the principles of multicultural and diversity education in all possible forms: "diversity training" alone will not be enough preparation as such training is really only one of the five categories of Sleeter's multiculturalism; all four others are essential for an adequate comprehension of the possibilities for multiculturalism. Team members or other groups working on curriculum reform must therefore experience for themselves over time a form of Banks's contributions, additive, transformation, and social action approaches, and discuss among themselves and with others the strengths and weakness of each. They must also be encouraged to push themselves beyond the most accessible and less threatening approaches. Incumbent upon the administration is the responsibility to build into budgets and long-range planning the time and resources that enable members of the community to continue to assess, evaluate, and reconsider practices and potential options beyond initial planning phases for at least five to seven years.

Comparing Lesson and Unit Plans

A common approach to curriculum reform for multicultural and diversity education is to take common lesson and unit plans and compare them with plans that cover the same traditional curricular content but also attend to issues of multiculturalism and diversity. After studying examples of such lessons, curriculum planning teams meet collaboratively to modify their own lesson and unit plans in the same ways. It is helpful to brainstorm a common set of encounters to which the lesson and unit plans will respond. For example, Sleeter and Grant (1999) list the following situations as a guide in thinking about planning lessons that take the "teaching the culturally different" approach:

> You have a new student who recently moved to the United States from Laos. She speaks only a handful of English words, and her life experiences are quite different from yours as well as from the other students' in the class.
>
> Three of your students spend a portion of their school day in learning disabilities classes. One of the students attends a class for the emotionally disturbed, and the other two are visually impaired.
>
> Most of the students in your class are Mexican Americans (and you are not). Some of their manners of responding to you are unfamiliar to you.
>
> You are transferred to a new school and most of your students live at or below the poverty level, unlike the socioeconomic background with which you are most familiar.
>
> A group of students in your class seems tuned out, unmotivated, and academically behind. (11)

The point of making such a list is not to generate a feeling of insurmountable odds against which the school must fight day in and day out, but to embrace the contexts of learning and teaching in one's school as the particularly unique and exciting challenges that characterize what it means to be a professional in one's school. Administrators and teachers often fall into the trap of thinking that they could do their job very well "if only . . . "; the attitude is one of despair about the obstacles to the perfect school or classroom situation. The multicultural response is to avoid such desperation in favor of a recognition that teaching and learning means teaching and learning about all of the children in the school, and working with all of the members of the community.

Teaching the Exceptional and Culturally Different

Nevertheless, the kind of list that Sleeter and Grant include demonstrates that any approach of teaching the exceptionally and culturally different shares a common characteristic: one or more of the students differ from the teacher's or school's conception of what is "normal" or generally expected. In this type of situation, standard routines and strategies do not work or do not function well. For example, students may not be able to read the material that the teacher is accustomed to using, or they may find the material uninteresting and irrelevant to their own experiences and goals. Students may speak a language or dialect foreign to the teacher and sometimes use this language when the teacher feels that they should use Standard English. Students may appear to be "acting out" when the teacher does not expect it, but the students themselves may not see themselves as acting out. A teacher may think she has planned motivating activities but some students may not be motivated by them. Students may talk or whisper when the teacher expects silence; they may sit passively when a discussion is supposed to be taking place.

This traditional approach recognizes that students may be exceptional or culturally different. "Exceptional" is often used to refer to students in special education or gifted programs, but this term can also refer to any student who is not succeeding academically. "Culturally different" refers to students whose cultural background (race, ethnicity, language, social class, sexual orientation) differs from that of the teacher. The term also implies that there is sufficient cultural difference between the teacher and the students that there is no longer effective teaching and learning. This can happen even if the teacher and students share a language, race, or other culturally significant characteristic; and it does not necessarily happen when the teacher and students different racially or ethnically. The long-term goals of this approach, however, are to enable the students to succeed in the traditional curriculum in traditional classrooms, and to be successful in the existing society, without attending to larger social, cultural, or political issues of diversity and pluralism.

In comparing existing and redesigned lessons and units, attention should be paid to ideas about differing learning styles, the inclusion of activities that are accessible to students of varying skill levels, and the development of caring relationships between staff and students. Varying modalities of instructional delivery and classroom organization should be a component of redesign as well. Independent of the district approach to language and issues of English-only instruction, it is also strongly suggested that students be encouraged to speak with each other in a first language if possible in formulating concepts and ideas before translating their discussion into English or presenting a group's experience or product to an audience in English.

Teaching the exceptional and culturally different raises concerns for some people. It should be expected that teachers will find it hard to imagine how to include students whom they perceive as "different" in their plans, and that other students and the students' families may resent the time and attention given to the exceptional and different students. Such a response is inconsistent with a pluralist approach to education and undermines multicultural values, so it is a tremendous obstacle to successful curriculum change. Political attention to these concerns should focus on the research support for improved academic performance for *all* students that results from such learning environments. The preparation for working with diverse groups of people that such multicultural education provides is also an advantage in a competitive job market. Broader work with the community is necessary to develop a better sense of the contributions and interests of all members of the community in order to promote supportive pluralist intergroup communication beyond the school. Administrators themselves may not be comfortable with the amount of talking and moving around that is necessary in a pluralist classroom; it behooves an administrator to visit schools that are successfully meeting similar goals, and to speak with the principals and staff of these schools about how they were able to adjust to new expectations for classroom management and discipline. This is also an opportunity to discuss alternative assessment strategies, cross-grade programs, and other nontraditional curricular structures.

Human Relations Approach

The human relations approach is directed toward developing respect among individuals of varying races, genders, classes, abilities, and sexual orientations. Respect for oneself and others, positive student-student relationships, elimination of stereotypes about others, improved self-concept (especially related to individual and cultural differences), and positive cross-group communication are the key goals. Common techniques include cooperative and collaborative learning; direct curricular attention to attitudes, prejudices, and stereotypes; personal feelings and values clarification; individual uniqueness and worth through lessons that foster pride in one's own accomplishments; and cross-group communication. Incorporating these techniques in lessons and units can be a proactive response that avoids potential cross-group tensions and misunderstandings.

Situations that may suggest a human relations approach:

> A mainstreamed student who uses a wheelchair finds that none of the other students speak to her on her first day in class. Instead they giggle and stare when they think she is not looking.
>
> It is November and a visitor to a fourth-grade classroom asks one of the students about the project three other students are working on in the corner. The student shrugs and says he doesn't know their names because they are not in his reading group.
>
> The Italian American and African American students inhabit the same facilities and classrooms in your high school, but rarely mix or talk with each other. When they do mix their interactions are superficial. Occasional fights and verbal insults occur.
>
> Some of the Latino students refuse to acknowledge their ability to speak Spanish; they seem embarrassed by their parents and their Spanish surnames that suggest they know Spanish. Other Latino students clearly take pride in the culture and language and are offended by their Latino brothers and sisters who act "white." They also resent white classmates who avoid them.
>
> Girls and boys rarely play together at recess. Sometimes boys laugh off girls who want to join them, saying they are not good enough at what they are playing. A few boys mock the less athletic boys, calling them "sissies" and "fags." (Adapted from Sleeter and Grant 1999, 56)

It may be difficult to establish and maintain cross-group communication in the classroom, and it may seem like school personnel do not have the training to effectively lead cross-group discussion. However, schools have some advantages that other organizations do not have. The teacher is in charge, and students typically assume the teacher's authority. They may look up to the teacher, often respect her or him, and generally believe that the teacher thinks she or he is doing something with the students' best interests at heart, even when they find the teacher's behaviors culturally offensive. If the teacher works with the students to develop a classroom that is open, civil, and honest, then the classroom can become a safe place for frank discussion and the sharing of ideas.

There are several characteristics of teachers who are excellent at establishing cross-group communication in classes made up of several different kinds of groups. They use a variety of techniques and strategies, including cooperative learning. They specifically teach the communication skills of listening, sharing, inviting, getting one's point across, and respecting other opinions. They also explicitly teach about cultural differences in communication styles, which allows students of different backgrounds to more correctly interpret each other. Lessons about communication involve factual information about communication skills and styles, demonstrations of communication skills, role-playing, and contact with people whose communication skills differ from the students' skills. These techniques can and should be integrated throughout the curriculum, as part of the principle that communication is central to mathematics, language arts, science, social studies, the arts, and other areas of the curriculum. To be effective, communication skills cannot be isolated lessons but must be a regular and routine part of the daily curriculum.

Single-Group Studies

Supporters of single-group studies seek a reduction in social stratification, and hope to raise the status of the group on which they focus. They promote immediate recognition of the identified group. Programs should present a more accurate version of U.S. history and culture by including groups and perspectives that have been left out of the stories. They should meet economic, political, and cultural demands by people of color from both within and outside of local communities. They should support intellectual inquiries into the political and historical forces affecting the group, and they should eliminate or reduce white racism.

This approach is a direct response to the school's goal of promoting a willingness and knowledge among students to work toward social change that would benefit the identified group. It is also used to develop a general social advocacy attitude that can be extended to other identifiable groups. Units and courses about the culture of an identified group focus on how that group has been victimized, examine current social issues facing the group (from the perspective of that group), and integrate traditional subject matter only from the perspective of the group's history and culture. Instruction builds on students' learning styles, and especially nurtures learning styles common within the identified cultural group. School learning environments are designed and decorated to reflect the culture and history of the group, and scheduled guest speakers and cultural events coincide with topics in the curriculum. The school makes a commitment to employ faculty and staff who are members of the group being studied.

In many ways, single-group studies is the most conservative approach to multicultural and diversity education because it is primarily a content-driven curriculum reform effort. Faculty and staff must prepare by learning the content themselves in order to implement the curriculum. The main curricular effort is spent in restructuring the "canon," what Lauter (1991) has described as the set of literary works, the grouping of philosophical, political, and religious texts, and the particular accounts of history generally accorded cultural weight within society. Because an oppressed group has been so consistently portrayed from the perspective of groups other than their own, it is a challenge to understand the culture and history "from within," and to genuinely present the material of the curriculum in this way. Ongoing assessment attentive to this issue is essential in order to avoid an unintentional propagation of inappropriate interpretations or inadvertent silencing of stories and ideas. It is also helpful to persistently work at instructional strategies that are culturally congruent with the group under study.

Advocates of single-group studies are concerned with the processes of socialization and deculturation inherent in the daily experience of schools. Research about stages of identity development that differ between dominant and nondominant people of color support these curricular responses. Students and teachers who are members of dominant groups are typically in the stage of encapsulation. They have been taught that people like themselves have run this country since its earliest history, and have contributed to its greatest achievements. This arrogant message leads to the feeling that there is no need to understand oppression or the experiences of the oppressed. The idea of "oppression" may be incomprehensible; these people believe their society is free and open to all, and see no need to change any school practices.

Single-group studies move students to higher levels. Powerful information about discrimination can have a strong impact on students and teachers. For oppressed-group members, the lowest stage is conformity. Dominant group members are most comfortable with conformists, because they are accepting. For example, white teachers tend to be more comfortable with minority students who accept the

Table 3.1 Stages of Identity Development

Dominant Group	Oppressed Group
Autonomy. Work actively to end discrimination against oppressed group; have positive identity with own but not accepting of own group's superior status.	*Commitment.* Committed to long-term work on antidiscrimination strategies; positive identity with one's own group and with members of dominant group who are in autonomy.
Pseudo-Independence. Resolving disintegration by actively seeking information about other group by contacting them or hanging around with its members; identify more with other group than one's own.	*Internalization.* Strong positive identity with own group. Willing to reconnect with dominant group but not with subordinate status.
Reintegration. Resolving disintegration by returning as best as possible to encapsulation.	*Resistance and Immersion.* Actively rejecting dominant society and its beliefs; increased desire to learn about own group.
Disintegration. Confronting evidence of discrimination that clashes with previous perspective; guilt, anger.	*Dissonance.* Confronting evidence of discrimination that clashes with previous perspective; confusion, wants more knowledge.
Encapsulation. Comfortable with status quo; do not think much about other groups' experiences or perspectives; accepts society's stereotypes of others.	*Conformity.* Identity with dominant group and its version of society; accepts negative images of one's own group.

Sleeter and Grant 1999, p. 121.

teacher's authority and a white-dominated curriculum; these teachers often become uncomfortable with students who assert their racial identity. Dissonance and disintegration are often the result of personal experiences that cannot be reflected in the curriculum, or new information that directly confronts something that one has learned. This can lead to wanting to know more and further growth.

When planning single-group studies, it is important to decide how the curriculum will relate to the rest of the school program. A separate approach can be superficial without well-thought-out reasons for the separation, resulting in little in-depth study of the group itself, and the employment of poor instructional strategies. This can happen, for example, with ethnic festivals, group-studies weeks or themes, food, and folk sharing. Advocates of single-group studies recommend integrating the program into the content of the mainstream curriculum. Otherwise the single-group study is supplementary to the perceived authentic curriculum. In this way, information about the group's historical and cultural experiences is made a natural component of the traditional content. Critics of this approach stress the pressure to adapt the study to the organization of the traditional disciplinary curriculum whether or not it is appropriate to the group being studied. When content about the group is absorbed into courses taught by individuals who are not trained in the study of that group, there is a real danger that the experiences of the marginalized will be marginalized even more.

Multicultural Education (Cultural Democracy)

The multicultural education approach seeks to reform the entire process of schooling for all students. Unlike the teaching-exceptionally-and-culturally-different-students approach, this way of rethinking the school curriculum is not just for certain groups of students. It is for everybody, and it seeks not only to integrate people into our existing society but also to improve society for all. Unlike the human relations approach, the multicultural education approach does not stop with the improvement of attitudes but works to develop skills and a strong knowledge base that will support an ideological commitment to multiculturalism. Unlike the single-group studies approach, it works to change more about schooling than just the content and instructional processes of the curriculum. Sonia Nieto (1996) describes multicultural education as a process of school reform that "permeates the curriculum and instructional strategies used in schools, as well as the interactions among teachers, students, and parents, and the very way that schools conceptualize the nature of teaching and learning" (6).

Cultural pluralism means that there is no best way to be a member of society. Equal opportunity means that each student is given equal opportunity to learn, succeed, and become what he or she would like with full affirmation of his or her gender, race, social class background, sexual orientation, and/or disability. Equal opportunity also requires an exploration of power and privilege, and whether or not power and privilege are implicitly accepted as invisible norms (rights) of a dominant group, inadvertently marginalizing other groups.

Curriculum materials and content should be identified to reflect multiple and divergent perspectives, engaging all students in learning the different subjects in the curriculum, and attending to issues of diversity including gender issues, ethnicity issues, issues of sexuality, and other diversity issues. Curricula should connect with the social context of the students in the school and attend to their interests and experiences. Information can be obtained from curriculum specialists and resource centers in school districts; librarians in public and school libraries; local students, parents, and community members; multicultural bookstores; and the resources mentioned in Chapters 7 and 8 of this book. Multiple perspectives should be a component of instructional practices as well as curriculum content. Teachers should be attentive to the possibility of a wide range of learning styles and personal interests, providing the opportunity to work with members of diverse groups and fostering awareness of communication issues that arise when members of different groups come together to form a community.

Evaluation should include multiple forms of assessment and avoid norm-referenced tests that are designed to compare and rank students against a biased standard. A more productive, multicultural approach to evaluation determines which students need further instruction and in what areas, and then implements that instruction. As many participants in the process as possible should monitor multiple forms of assessment in order to identify potential hazards for diversity. Students should not be penalized for lacking skills that are a part of what has been taught; this means that students should be given ample time, they should be encouraged to speak if they cannot write, they should be encouraged to spell correctly but not be penalized for misspelling if they are not being tested on spelling; and they should be given the opportunity to demonstrate what they have learned collaboratively or in unconventional formats if at all possible.

Relationships with parents should be broadened into a genuine collaboration with the community. Teachers systematically learn about the community's history, learn about their students' homes and where people in the community go for entertainment and social events, visit local organizations and religious institutions, read the local newspapers, and participate in neighborhood activities. They communicate personally with parents and share teaching duties with parents rather than managing parent involvement. Joint activities with other institutions in the community should be planned as integral components of the curriculum. Often, home and community relationships are discussed as "partnerships" without exploring why members of a community feel and act as they do. Sometimes people view multiculturalism as a harmonizing agent rather than a democratizing agent. Conflicts arise, and they should be expected and respected as part of cultural pluralism. Students, teachers, administrators, and community members need to examine why community groups take the positions that they do take and how certain groups and workers within a community may be affected by policy decisions made by that community.

Education That Is Multicultural and Social Reconstructionist

Multicultural and social reconstructionist curricula promote equity and cultural pluralism by preparing citizens to work actively toward social structural equality, by promoting cultural pluralism and supporting alternative lifestyles, and by promoting equal opportunity in the school. Content is organized around current social issues involving racism, classism, sexism, ablism, and so on. Concepts are organized around experiences and perspectives of culturally different groups. Extrapolations to global issues of equity and pluralism include perspectives from cultures and nations that challenge the status quo and assumptions of the students, teachers, administrators, and community members. Students' life experiences become the starting point for analyzing oppression, developing and refining critical thinking skills, subtly analyzing alternative viewpoints, building social action skills, and acquiring empowerment. Students are actively involved in democratic decision making that builds on students' varying learning styles. Cooperative and collaborative learning structures adapt to students' skill levels and support the commitment to a diverse student body.

> Goals that suggest multicultural and social reconstructionist curricula:
> Students should be informed and aware of issues and problems in the world. They should approach the world with eyes wide open, noticing things that are wrong or unfair, alert to injustices and inequities.
> Students should feel a commitment to making a difference. They should have a sense that what they do matters, that they can make a difference, and that they must be willing to expend the energy and time to do so.
> Students should have the skills and strategies they need in order to take on problems and issues. They must have communication skills (talking to others, asking questions, and listening), information gathering skills (reading, data gathering, and ways to sort through confusing or conflicting information), conflict resolution skills (what to do when people don't agree or are getting angry), and skills in bringing about change (letter writing, lobbying, and advocacy). (Sapon-Shevin 1999, 157)

Schoolwide concerns are an important component of education that is multicultural and social reconstructionist. Students should be involved in democratic decision making about substantive schoolwide concerns and policies. Lower-class and racially diverse parents are actively involved in school activities. The school uses local community action projects as a substantial and integrated component of the curriculum. Staffing patterns include diverse racial, gender, and disability groups in nontraditional roles. Disciplinary procedures do not penalize any one group more than any other. All areas of the school building are accessible to all. Decision making does not rely on "majority rule," but recognizes that minority opinions can be substantive and important to the democratic perpetuation of the community.

Sleeter and Grant characterize the multicultural and social reconstructionist approach as growing out of a wide-ranging collective of advocates who do not always agree on all of their practices. The result, they write, is a hodgepodge of scattered practitioners that makes it hard to build coalitions. It is difficult to find resources that explicitly speak to this approach, leaving the educator to put together aspects of the other approaches that support a vision. Often this approach is ignored by people who view it as too radical or too advanced. Some think the goals are too glorious and are beyond the scope of schools. Those who seek to help the exceptionally and culturally different feel this way; they want change for those who are disempowered *now*, not work for some fantasy future. Others are bewildered by the contradictions between telling students to think for themselves and persuading them to think like the teachers. This can lead to a kind of paralysis that makes it too challenging to do either.

Students lack experience with this approach, which of course is the fault of their schooling experiences; but this lack of experience makes the prospect of a small group of educators working in isolation a daunting task. It is frustrating to lead students into awareness but then to have a difficult time figuring out ways for them to act on their awareness in fulfilling ways. Often, students can be accidentally taught that they have *no* power to effect change if their efforts are unsuccessful and go uncritiqued. This makes curriculum planning and implementation seem too complex for some educators, or too complex for some students.

It is also very challenging to build coalitions when one is also seeking to address conflicts among groups, typically for the first time. Human relations educators are especially concerned about anything that could aggravate conflict and tension. Multiculturalists have such a hard time implementing their cultural democracy approaches that they cannot imagine working toward the goals of social reconstructionist education. To the advocates of the social reconstructionist approach, all of the others are not assertive enough. Other approaches do more harm than good by setting up a hidden curriculum that teaches students that society is set up well and needs only minor tinkering to be fair to all of its members. Of course some people believe this. But they tend to be white, upper-middle-class people who have not reflected on the issues that lead to a multicultural point of view in the first place.

The fact that schools have not traditionally taught social action skills makes it more difficult to see these skills as an important part of the school curriculum. Advocates of a social reconstructionist approach note that putting traditional skills and content in the context of social action meets the traditional goals of education more effectively anyway, by making the content and skills relevant and meaningful to the students.

Critical Multiculturalism

A serious critique even of the social reconstructionist approach to multiculturalism is that it "essentializes" categories of people, and this criticism is made by those both on the left and right politically. For example, many schools

> have been developing literature curricula to meet the needs of their culturally diverse students. However, because in most cases these educators have not had at their disposal the interpretative techniques of postcolonial literary theorists, they have been relying, instead, for their reading strategies upon traditional literary theories. Unfortunately, when teachers employ New Critical, archetypal, feminist, or reader-response methods of literary analysis in their reading of multicultural literature, they are often unaware of the Eurocentric biases contained within these perspectives. This lack of understanding of their theoretical frame of reference can then lead teachers to encourage their students to accept uncritically problematic representations of various cultural groups as they encounter these representations in their literary texts. Postcolonial literary theory, on the other hand, encourages students to problematize Eurocentric representations of imperialism's Others. (Greenlaw 1995)

Postmodern theories in general require us to reconsider the notion of identity, and to realize that people "travel" in and out of multiple groups and identities all of the time. In a way, it is an old-fashioned view of schools that sees collections of microgroups in conflict or entrenched in self-perpetuating relationships of power and oppression. This does not mean that oppression is not real, or that inequalities cannot be identified across social groups. But what we need to do is to develop theories and practices that can respond to the realities of how individuals experience group identities and social relationships in their everyday lives in and out of school, and to think about what this means for how educators can and should respond.

Attention to youth cultures and the sorts of experiences that are integral to growing up in the United States at the beginning of the twenty-first century helps us to see that young people are comfortable with, and expect, fluidity and multiplicity in their identities and coalitions. They also accept conflicts among these identities as part of "performing their identity." MTV, cable programming, Internet surfing, and hypermedia entertainment create a world in which identity is *performed*. Diane Dubose Brunner (1998) writes that the performance of identity acknowledges and makes visible the social masks that have allowed multiple constructions to remain invisible. When we recognize that identity is performed in constantly shifting and paradoxical ways, we can begin to see the processes of identity-making, identity-marking, and the parallel processes that work to create a sense of "fixity" in identities. This is a whole new language of multiculturalism, distinct from the modernist sense of group cultures and social dynamics that informed the majority of decisions and curricular innovations that came before it. This "position" neither denies fixity nor suggests it, but instead works to comprehend the relationships among difference and construction as ideas that inform our ways of making meaning. It is more of an orientation than an approach.

Pedagogy in this kind of critical multicultural diversity education offers no final answers, because it cannot presume to speak for all people away from the actual people who must create the community of which it hopes to speak. Instead, this approach tries to help people in schools to understand reality itself as a process of making meaning, the realities we "see" in our school as the ways in which we comprehend possibilities, and our practices as a sort of "theater of identity performance." The lack of "answers," however, does not make the approach less useful or effective. Rather, it makes the search for final answers a nonissue as the members of the school community work together toward social justice and equity. When people are working toward such goals, one can often say that the school is effectively implementing a multicultural diversity change process. The curricular reform suggested by this approach is to adopt this new language of critique for all concerned—teachers, students, administrators, and community members. Because it is not intertwined with all of the rhetoric of group conflicts and group identities, this new language holds the prospect of being independent of all of the politics that have prevented multiculturalism from making a genuine difference in the lives of students and teachers. Because it is directly concerned with the relationships that people create with the language of identities and the performance of self, it holds a promise of relevance to students' lives and the social communities of which they are a part.

Advocates of a critical multicultural curriculum work first to "untell" essentialism, and to develop strategies that undermine essentialist hierarchies. They work to open up for students and teachers the fluidity of identity and possibilities for their own lives that can also be used to interrogate the received stories about history and culture that come in the prepackaged curricula and materials available to them in and out of school. A central feature of this orientation is a persistent effort on the part of teachers and students to always look at how people are represented as "types" or categories, and how these types and categories lead to implications that directly affect their own identities, how they perform their identities for others in varying contexts.

Critical multiculturalists will critique the curriculum that they study with their students. They will also study experiences of popular culture as parallel forms of "representation." They study with students how the school curriculum and popular cultural forms of entertainment and information define an "order of things" for people—how to dress, how to eat, what to want, and in general how to be in the world. Instead of searching for the best curricular materials or designing the best units of study, critical multiculturalists look for "interventions" (by which they mean points in the curriculum, moments in classroom interactions, places in the community or the school) where they can disrupt the representations, or where they can see the diverse locations of the multiple identities that are part of what they are studying (part of what they are doing together). Sometimes, as in the case of Brunner, they playfully talk about "in(ter)ventions" (102), so that they can see themselves and their students as simultaneously, on the spot, inventing new ways to do things together in school and out of school; they use words like this and play with them to provoke themselves and each other to think about how an intervention might also be an invention, how an invention of ways of talking or representing what they know might itself be an intervention into the inequities and problems of social life.

Critical Pedagogy for Diversity Education

What critical multiculturalism seeks to achieve is a way to avoid all of the problems that self/other categories create for schools and societies.

A reference work like this one is asked to reduce people and ideas to a simple, straightforward, and coherent collection of information. It turns out the key to the meaningful implementation of multicultural and diversity education, however, is more complex. Content strategy and cultural materials are important to the curriculum, as are democratic processes in the classroom. But crucial to the success of diversity education is that we teach about issues of knowledge and power and about the politics of schooling. Teachers' roles within the hierarchies that are established by the ways that people are represented in the media, school curricula, and actions that create the teacher-student relationship in the school all need to be analyzed by teachers, by teachers and administrators together in safe groups, and most importantly by the students themselves. The students must further analyze their own actions in setting up categories that become "essentialized" as unchanging sets of assumptions and stereotypes.

Critical pedagogy for diversity addresses throughout the school curriculum the contingencies of consumer culture and how they make the transformation of society so difficult. It explicitly studies the politics of education, the politics of representation in the curriculum and in popular culture, and it makes all of this a part of educating for a democracy. Ethics become central, set up as responsible action (both collective and individual). Teachers meet to discuss how their students make meanings and how these meanings figure into the formation of nonessentialized identities, which assumes a political assessment of the ways that cultures are represented. Students and teachers study the interactions in the school themselves as "texts" to understand. Everything becomes a possible text for analysis by students of all ages, even the behaviors they observe or do not observe.

Border Literacies

The job of critical diversity educators is to enable themselves and students to formulate new languages about differences among people, and about what identities are. Another way to phrase this is to say that the job is to "defeat representation," because all representation leads to viewing people as "self" and "other." This process of "othering people" is what leads to views of people as different and potentially unequal. At first glance this orientation may seem to have a lot in common with the human relations approach. But even the human relations approach sets up people as different in order to help us learn about how and why they are different. This orientation helps teachers and students to speak differently about people. To adopt the language of the orientation requires a new way of thinking, a way of thinking that translates commonalities that might be found across differences in the human relations approach into collectivities of people that could be the basis of coalitions. In this way everyone is seen to be a part of many overlapping communities and groups. Some of the groups may be overtly or subtly conflicting; but still, each person is a member of these groups, and so each person has multiple identities. With everyone performing multiple identities all at once, there are no clear boundaries among groups, even as collectivities may call for attention to the needs of a particular group. Trinh T. Minha (1989) writes, "Trying to find the other by defining otherness or by explaining the other through laws and generalities is, as Zen says, like beating the moon with a pole or scratching an itching foot from the outside of the shoe" (75).

When we talk about new languages, we are speaking about literacy; and when we search for ways to avoid essentializing the categories we have for people, and to recognize the multiplicities of each person's identities, we are speaking about blurring the boundaries. For example, homi bhaba works to "estrange" home cultures and home identities (bhaba 1994, 9). Judith Butler (1993), too, writes about redefining home in "other" terms; she redefines home as "not solely that of whiteness or heterosexual terms, and in all its forms of collectivity" (240). Bhaba describes this as "displacing essentialism," as the "unhomely moment when the borders between home and world become confused, and uncannily, the public and the private become part of each other, forcing us into a vision that is as divided as it is disorienting" (9). The term for these kinds of literacy is "border literacies," referring to the blurring of the boundaries between home and other identities, and the fact that people are always treading the blurred borders between. We are never "in" any one identity. Instead, outside identities are part of the inside identities of home, and inside identities are part of the outside identities. We always exist in the ambiguous borderland of overlapping identities, where we could not say which side of what borders we are on. Imagine a no-man's land where one might claim any single identity at any one moment. Border literacies find common multicultural practices too limiting because they do not explore the borderlands of identity. Unsophisticated approaches to diversity shift marginal voices and minority groups to the center of our attention, and move the dominant voices to the margins. Border literacy approaches put aside the insider/outsider boundaries, and search for the ways in which insider identities are formed through the interaction of the marginal identities, and how the outsider identities are formed through the othering practices of the insider identities. Critical multicultural curricula foster border literacies by providing experiences that serve as interventions rather than as lessons to be learned, and in the process, promote those sorts of skills and funds of knowledge that enable participants to more fully enact a multicultural democracy.

REFERENCES AND FURTHER READING

bhaba, homi. 1994. *The Location of Culture.* New York: Routledge.

Brunner, Diane Dubose. 1998. *Between the Masks: Resisting the Politics of Essentialism.* Lanham, MD: Rowman and Littlefield.

Butler, Judith. 1993. *Bodies That Matter: On the Discursive Limits of "Sex."* New York: Routledge.

Greenlaw, Jim. 1995. "A Postcolonial Conception of the High School Multicultural Literature Curriculum." Saskatchewan School Trustees Association Web site, http://www.ssta.sk.ca/research/students/95-05.htm.

Kincheloe, Joe, and Shirley Steinberg. 1997. *Changing Multiculturalism: New Times, New Curriculum.* New York: Open University Press.

Lauter, Paul. 1991. *Canons and Contexts.* New York: Oxford University Press.

Mahalingam, Ram, and Cameron McCarthy. 2000. *Multicultural Curriculum: New Directions for Social Theory, Practice, and Policy.* New York: Falmer Press.

Nieto, Sonia. 1996. *Affirming Diversity: The Sociopolitical Context of Multicultural Education.* New York: Longman.

Sapon-Shevin, Mara. 1999. *Because We Can Change the World: A Practical Guide to Building Cooperative, Inclusive Classroom Communities.* Boston: Allyn & Bacon.

Sleeter, Christine, and Carl Grant. 1998. *Turning on Learning: Five Approaches for Multicultural Teaching—Plans for Race, Class, Gender, and Disability.* Upper Saddle River, NJ: Merrill.

———. 1999. *Making Choices for Multicultural Education: Five Approaches to Race, Class, and Gender.* Upper Saddle River, NJ: Merrill.

Trinh T. Minha. 1989. *Woman, Native, Other: Writing, Postcoloniality, and Feminism.* Bloomington: Indiana University Press.

Chapter Four

•• Case Studies

Because there are so many questions regarding the variety of curricular approaches to multicultural and diversity education, this chapter explores a sample of instructional and philosophical approaches that some schools and organizations are pursuing. These curricular and instructional approaches vary from school to organization, reflecting the diverse educational philosophies that underlie the options for multicultural and diversity education, and the community contexts in which they function. A brief and general overview of the curriculum approaches and instructional philosophies of some schools and organizations will provide insight into how many are constructing their educational designs and curriculum.

Given the questions that critical multiculturalism raises regarding representation, it is difficult to present the stories in a consistent manner. Instead, each unique story will provide an example of the ideological perspective of the approach as well as what we have referred to as an "untelling" of the essentializing narratives of cultural and other identities.

WESTVIEW DISTRICT'S EDUCATION
FOR AN INTEGRATED COMMUNITY

The Westview school district sees multicultural and diversity education as a prime element of its efforts to be a leading model of a successful integrated and socioeconomically diverse school district. In this suburban community, all schools are magnet schools with themes. Families and students can choose an elementary and middle school based on the type of education they believe is best for the student and the sort of family involvement that they expect in a school. There are six elementary options, three middle-school options, and one comprehensive high school. Choice of magnet school is accomplished by a partial lottery that ensures that each school is ethnically and racially diverse in its student population. Because schools are entirely magnet-based, the community is increasingly diverse and integrated: few people select a home based on the school their child will attend as is common in suburban school districts. Hiring takes into account the district's goal of a school staff that models a successfully integrated community. The high school is introducing themed school-within-a-school curricula to accomplish the same diversity successes of the elementary and middle-school populations. Special programs for all students at the elementary level avoid the need for "teaching the culturally different"; for example, a writer's room program staffed by community volunteers serves all students, not those targeted as needing special assistance or as gifted in some way, but all students who are working on writing assignments in their school programs. Much of the curriculum is typical of the contributions approach and occasionally multicultural/cultural democracy. Teachers go out of their way to research all possible ethnic, racial, and religious expectations, interests, and events, and to make them a part of their classroom practices. No members of any group are expected to explain what they need or want from the school; and routine assessment of the comfort of diverse subgroups of the population gauges how well the schools are accomplishing their goals of including and valuing all members of the community. Cross-age and mixed-grade activities are used as weekly problem-based interdisciplinary learning in all of the elementary schools; daily in some of them. Students choose from a limited selection that is based on the school's theme—for example, internationalism; family and the environment; community and technology; Montessori education. In the gifted-and-talented themed magnet, all children experience a gifted-and-talented curriculum. In studying Native American culture, the district invites Native Americans to speak about history and culture from their own personal experience rather than to represent Native American culture through a received meta-narrative in a social studies textbook. The presence of African American and Latino cultures from an African American or Latino perspective is used in assessment of all curricular programs.

Middle schools carry the district emphasis on diversity education into social action and a careful deconstruction of the ways in which contemporary society perpetuates stereotypes and inequities. For example, middle-school students study race relations in the community by grounding their investigation in their own personal stories of discrimination and privilege. The history of race relations in the United States is interpreted in light of these personal stories, and through literature chosen to be compared with the students' own stories. Students then take their conclusions to the community and interview members of the community on issues that emerge as central to their discussions; in one year they might question local business owners and patrons about the racial tensions in the community and their impact on the local economy. A local jazz musician leads a school's saxophone "choir," and works with students and the art teacher on curatorship projects; and students choose race-related issues for their science projects and theater projects. Peer-mediation training is coupled with oral history projects on racial tensions in the community, with increasing responsibility for community application in each middle-school grade. In the sixth grade, the focus is mostly on developing mediation strategies that work, and familiarity with the recent history of racial interaction in the community; in the seventh grade, students work with the new sixth graders on mediation skills while understanding the national and international context of the oral histories they wrote in the previous year; in eighth grade, students challenge the successes of peer mediation in resolving conflicts, and explore other alternatives, while joining adults in the community for race-relations discussion groups held weekly for at least six months.

The ninth grade has its own special program housed in a separate building across the street from the rest of the high school. After much controversy, the district successfully "detracked" its ninth-grade language arts program and instituted a mixed-ability world literature curriculum. This curriculum builds on earlier middle-school discussions of students' personal experiences with race in an integrated community, and places these discussions more rigorously in the context of U.S. history and world literatures.

Yet there are clear indicators that this curriculum is "not yet enough." The district is consistently searching for ways to "close the gap" in test scores between white and nonwhite students. Yet they rarely examine the rhetoric of test scores and the discourse of accountability for its biases and harmful effects on integrated communities. Statistics persistently demonstrate overrepresentation of nonwhite students in the few remedial programs, on lists of behavior problems, and in special education programs, despite the socioeconomic range across race and ethnicity in this community. African American and white parents often find themselves on opposite sides of debates about the best curriculum choice or in other discussions. Multiculturalism is often branded a "white" thing by some members of the African American community, as a collection of practices that perpetuates inequality rather than providing serious attention to the skills and knowledge that their children need to receive in school. And there is consistent white-flight in the upper grades to private schools that have fancier facilities or more academic curricula, so that the population shifts from 60 percent white in the elementary schools to 60 percent African American in the high school. So Westview is making efforts to introduce multicultural education, but is doing very little to achieve diversity education or critical multicultural education at the district level.

TECHNOLOGY IN A FIFTH-GRADE CLASSROOM

John Weaver and Karen Grindall (1998) enact a "critical technomania" in their fifth grade classroom, with extensive use of the Internet and creative hypertext software. Using technology they reconfigure their classroom so that the teacher is no longer the lecturer or controller, becoming a "fellow traveler leaving bodies behind, traveling to worlds different from that of our modernist classrooms, and reaching goals that cannot be established the night before in a lesson plan" (242). With *Hollywood High,* a CD-ROM interactive storytelling program designed for elementary school children, this fifth grade class explores the re-creation of their identity through the stories they write and rewrite. Children are required by the software to create their story from constructing their own setting, choosing characters, determining the length of the story, inventing their own structure, and creating the identities of their own characters. The use of the software introduces an interesting interplay with limitations, on time, on possibilities, and on the assigned topics that the students explore with the software. For example, there are time restraints on using the program, topic restraints when Weaver and Grindall ask the students to create a story about the Underground Railroad or the extinction of the dinosaurs, and identity/character restraints imposed by the images and voices available in the software. Weaver and Grindall apply the work of Andrew Ross (1994), who has written, "most people tend to accept that 'limits,' whether they are socially imposed or socially chosen, are a necessary feature of any . . . reorganization of social life" (263–264). They make it possible in their classroom for students to question the limits as they morph the characters they create, and give nontraditional voices to assumed male or female characters. In resolving story lines, students are allowed and encouraged to reconsider their resolutions, often opting for presenting two or more conflicting perspectives; thus what actually happened can be left to the reader/viewer. Indeed, because students are given the latitude to question the notion of a fixed narrative structure, their use of *Hollywood High* provides them the opportunity to leave their story without an end or encapsulating privileged interpretation, exposes them to the idea of stories having more than one authorial voice, and affords them the opportunity to explore alternative identities within the stories they create. They can ask what the presence or absence of a certain character, ethnic perspective, historical awareness, or other factor does to change the nature of the story. In leaving stories open-ended, children are able to avoid a contrived consensus in which only one narrative or conclusion is possible. By turning males and females into hybrids, or attaching different voices to different appearances, they are able to form new identities that transcend the world of modern dichotomies and assumed fixed roles in society. Through this process, say Weaver and Grindall, the students are changed: they are no longer stationed in fixed categories such as male and female, past or present; students can move among them, constructing new markers that better capture the complexity, ambiguity, and contradictions of life.

In their use of the Internet following field experiences that constitute a spring unit on the environment, this class combines a focus on activism in their local community with global activism and international environmental issues. Concerned that the students not think that selling Blow Pops and soda for a good cause can solve environmental problems, Weaver and Grindall have their students share their concerns about the destruction and preservation of rivers throughout the world with the Environmental Center for Children in Braslavia. Via the Internet the children create their own environmental organization as they learn about other environmental problems beyond their local community. They develop initial activism skills that could be useful in assuring that the destruction of rivers does not continue.

"They became techno-activists developing a critical sense of environmental issues, and voicing their concerns about problems throughout the world without leaving the classroom. Being wired gave them access to issues they would not normally be made aware of, and it served as a conduit for action. The Internet transformed these students from future encyclopedia salespersons who began by selling Blow Pops into individuals who began to think of problems as global issues" (Weaver and Grindall 1998, 250).

INTERGENERATION ORCHESTRA OF OMAHA

Through their slogan, "Generations meeting on the Bridge of Music," the Intergeneration Orchestra blends the talents of musicians 22 and younger, and 55 and older, symbolized by their rose and bud logo; the "rose in bloom" represents the "lifetime of experience that older musicians bring to the group," while the "rosebud" signifies the "emerging talents of the younger artists." The Orchestra was founded in 1985 through a grant from the Peter Kiewit Foundation, with sponsorship of the Eastern Nebraska Office on Aging. "There are no minimum or maximum age restrictions in the ensemble." A recent year's Orchestra was composed of 55 musicians ranging in age from 11 to 75 years. "The Orchestra's concert season runs from September through April, with a schedule of 10 to 15 concerts. Performances are given for senior and retiree groups, at nursing homes, private events, conferences and schools. Community-wide events include annual fall and spring 'Pops & Pie' concerts at area performing arts venues."

"The Intergeneration Orchestra of Omaha is funded entirely through grants, donations, memberships, fundraisers and performance fees. The Orchestra is run by a Board of Directors that includes two elected younger and two elected older Orchestra musicians." In addition to musical performance, the Orchestra strives to build camaraderie among the musicians through "interaction" activities that take place at retreats and rehearsals. The goal of these exchanges is to help break down the barriers so that both generations better understand each other. "Since its founding, the Orchestra has toured nationally eight times—including two performances in Washington, D.C., Pittsburgh, Mount Rushmore, Bella Vista (Arkansas), Kansas City, Dallas, and Estes Park." An ongoing project is a multimedia artistic composition, "Ballet of Life," featuring music performed by the orchestra, dance, and video; the composition presents the concept that many aspects of daily work and play are "balletic" in their fluidity of motion.

As an intergenerational program, the Intergeneration Orchestra is exemplary because it combines interaction with social service and community involvement by engaging its participants in authentic curricular experiences. Their interest in performing for a variety of audiences is commendable. However, as a multicultural experience, the group could do far more to pursue diversity issues beyond generational issues. For example, they could explore the musical interests of their community beyond their current focus of orchestral "pops" concerts, bringing in local musicians who could contribute diverse cultural forms and styles to participate in the creation of their compositions. They could also combine their performances with exhibits by artists in their community to promote a multicultural awareness of the varieties of arts currently existing in their local community. These sorts of projects would reorient the group away from touring, which broadens the group members' understanding of communities outside their own, toward a focus on the diversity of cultures within their own community.

TWO DISTRICTS WORKING TOGETHER
ON MEDIA AWARENESS

Two teachers who met in a graduate course developed a media awareness program to enable their students to meet each other and to promote the study of how ethnicity is portrayed by the media. "Ms. Vaccaro" teaches social studies and language arts in an urban secondary school that is 85 percent African American and 15 percent Latino, and "Ms. Ammundson" teaches fourth grade in a nearby suburban elementary school that is 60 percent white, 25 percent Latino, 11 percent African American, and 4 percent Asian. They based their activities on materials available from the Canadian Media Awareness Network (http://www. media-awareness.ca/ eng/issues/minrep/resource/teachunt.htm), "Teaching Units on Portrayal of Diversity." First, each class spent a preparatory month studying stereotyping, perceptions of race, and critical knowledge of bias in information presented on television and the Internet using the Awareness Network's lessons, which are designed for elementary and secondary students respectively, with a weekly focus on the Network's lesson topics. In fourth grade, this included two weeks on stereotypes, another week on stereotype and bias using the story of the wolf and the three little pigs, a lesson on prejudicial information on the Internet; they prepared a kids' guide for grown-ups on how to talk with children about racial stereotypes based on a sample from the Network Web site. For the secondary students, the program included a week on spotting bias in newspaper and television reporting, a week on the underrepresentation of Native Americans and visible minorities in the media, another week developing ideas about the representation of minorities in reporting, and a final week studying how crime reporting affects people's attitudes about race and ethnicity. Groups of students e-mailed the students in the other school about what they were learning and what questions they still had remaining about media portrayal and possible bias in media coverage of race and ethnicity. The two teachers specifically chose to have the students e-mail each other about substantive curriculum content rather than to "get to know each other," in order to promote a sense of seriousness of purpose and to more easily meet their schools' expectations about meeting state curriculum content standards.

In the second month of their project, the students met weekly on Friday afternoons to discuss what they had been learning about and to design a collaborative investigation. They took turns meeting in each other's school, and touring the schools' surrounding communities. Part of each weekly meeting was devoted to screening a television program or viewing a Web site that the hosting class had chosen for discussion based on what they had been talking about in their group meetings, with either small group or whole group discussion. Originally, the teachers were concerned that the different ages of the students would make it hard for the secondary students to appreciate what the younger children had to offer. However, they found that the high schoolers were fascinated with the fourth graders' perspectives, and the fourth graders were always excited to learn from the older students, so that the mixed ages became a significant advantage.

Nearing the end of the second month, the students developed a collaborative project idea. They decided to create their own television program about how they themselves were learning about media portrayal of race and ethnicity, to be aired on local cable television stations. The teachers knew about an annual conference on media and education that invites submissions from students, and suggested that it might be possible to send the final product to this conference. The students agreed it would be exciting to get exposure beyond their local communities. They spent the next month of weekly meetings working in small mixed-age groups on different topics for their video program, coming together to present their developing ideas for their parts of the program, and to regularly discuss how the parts of the program would fit together. A fourth month was devoted to videotaping their documentary, and a final celebratory screening at each school, with families of the students attending both screenings if possible. The resulting video combined interviews of the two teachers and students themselves with a mock news program on "the portrayal of race and ethnicity in the media" that featured headline news, fashionable trends in the underrepresentation of minorities in the media, a "weather forecast" about the future of media bias, a sportslike comparison of Internet and television portrayal, bias and underrepresentation, and a special report on how coverage of crime affects public attitudes about race and ethnicity.

CAROL CORNELIUS AND
CULTURE-BASED CURRICULA

Carol Cornelius, area manager of the Oneida Cultural Heritage Department, Oneida Nation, has developed a way to research and develop curricula based on respect for diverse cultures. Using the Haudenosaunee culture as an example, she examines the sources and reasons for the prevailing stereotypes about American Indians and explains how those stereotypes became the standard curriculum being taught in the United States. She uses components of the Haudenosaunee worldview and how they structure a way of life—the interaction of corn and culture, the dynamic aspect of Haudenosaunee culture, and the contemporary role of corn—to weave the interdependent, holistic, interdisciplinary framework for a culture-based curriculum. Her approach serves as a model for beginning a multicultural curriculum process based on any culture.

Cornelius begins with three assumptions that guide the curriculum development work: that all cultures have fundamental value and integrity; that presenting cultures as holistically and culturally specific paradigms provides an in-depth view of a culture; and third, that all cultures are dynamic and changing. The third assumption is strategic in understanding that curriculum development must include extensive interaction with contemporary living history of the culture. Cornelius writes that we can find evidence of the dynamic nature of a culture in the contemporary or living history, in which the worldview continues to exist and guide contemporary lives and history. It is important to remember and recognize in the curriculum that cultures were dynamic before contact with other cultures. Selective adoption, the two-way exchange of cultural elements, continues to occur within the contemporary time period; this exchange happens in two directions whether we are discussing philosophies of democratic government or environmental issues, or using metal kettles instead of clay pots. Living history works to dispel the "primitive," "savage," and "vanishing race" stereotypes. More important, I would add, living history serves to dispel myths of cultural homogenization, in which stereotyping becomes the dominant mode of understanding various cultures. In speaking with elders, asking them to share their knowledge, young people have the opportunity to gain valuable knowledge and respect for our old ones, writes Cornelius; she also writes that the elders carry in their stories the culture's worldview. But the multiplicity of conflicting worldviews emerges in the current issues and events that can be examined to determine how the clash of worldviews impacts current problems and conflicts.

The culture-based curriculum requires study of (1) the worldview expressed by a particular culture; (2) the way the worldview is structured by the people's way of life, and enacted in the daily life of the culture; (3) the interaction of cultures; (4) the dynamic aspects of cultures, selective adoption/adaptations, and continuity of worldview; and (5) cultural continuity to contemporary times. Out of such research, curriculum development requires the identification of a thematic focus. Cornelius suggests that the thematic focus can be identified by asking people from the culture what they think should be taught about their culture. The focus should be a significant component of the interconnected web of relationships within the culture, so that it can be shown how the item or concept connects to the holistic worldview. An aspect of the culture becomes an artifact only when it is disconnected from its place within the web of relationships and taught separately. Using a thematic focus provides a way to counteract stereotypes of the culture by examining specific cultures as holistic entities.

Cornelius presents four criteria for developing culture-based curricula: (1) presenting multiple perspectives through a team approach; (2) selecting a thematic focus that emerges from the culturally specific paradigm; (3) utilizing an interdisciplinary approach; and (4) recognizing continuity of the culture into the contemporary era. The school team should contact people from the culture who are the best source of cultural knowledge, and include these people on the team of experts. The school team must include culture bearers not only to gather information but also as the authority on that information. Historical documents, oral traditions, newspapers, magazines, Web site publications by the culture, archival documents and pictures, old newspaper articles, and, most important, the views of contemporary elders and educators provide rich sources of materials. Using an interdisciplinary approach to teach about cultures is essential because the components of culture are interdependent. Cornelius warns that using isolated subject matter to teach components of a culture, such as might be common in many schools that teach about a culture in social studies, literature, art, science, and mathematics, can only lead to a fragmented view of that culture instead of an integrated, holistic view. Students would not interact with the culture in ways that could lead to understandings of the integral relationships within the entire culture.

Because Cornelius suggests that curriculum research should identify a cultural paradigm, she runs dangerously close to fostering a monolithic view of a cultural subgroup as stereotypically unified within a singular paradigm. Curriculum development that follows her work could potentially fall into the trap of transmitting hypersimplified views of cultural groups. Yet careful application of her ideas can also help educators to become familiar with the variety of subcultural conflicts and overlapping cultural ideas through interaction with a range of informants and resource materials. If the study of a cultural group is oriented in this manner, then students will benefit from the rich experience of understanding cultures as multifaceted and constantly reconstructing themselves in multiple ways.

BOB MOSES AND THE ALGEBRA PROJECT

The following description is reprinted with permission from the Algebra Project Web site:

 The Algebra Project is a national mathematics literacy effort aimed at helping low-income students and students of color—particularly African American students—successfully achieve mathematical skills that are a prerequisite for full citizenship in the Information Age. Founded by civil rights activist and math educator Robert Moses in the 1980s, the Algebra Project has developed curricular materials, trained teachers and trainers of teachers, and provided ongoing professional development support and community involvement activities to schools seeking to achieve a systemic change in mathematics education. The Algebra Project reaches approximately 10,000 students and approximately 300 teachers per year in 10 states and in 28 local sites, with a particular focus on the southern United States. Increased student performance in mathematics, as well as greater numbers of Algebra Project students enrolling in college preparatory mathematics classes, is a well-documented outcome of the organization's work. Graduates have formed a "Young Peoples' Project" that recruits, trains, and deploys high school and college-age youth to work with their younger peers in a variety of math learning opportunities and engage "the demand side" of mathematics education reform. The main goal of the Algebra Project is to impact the struggle for citizenship and equality by assisting students in inner-city and rural areas to achieve mathematics literacy. Higher-order thinking and problem-solving skills are necessary for entry into the economic mainstream. Without these skills children would be tracked into an economic underclass.

 The Algebra Project develops and implements curricular interventions that address a conceptual shift from arithmetic to algebraic thinking, by using experiences students find interesting—and understand intuitively—to open up the basic concepts of algebraic thinking. A ride on a subway, a trip on a bus, or a walking tour become bases for understanding displacements. Stories about "making do" become the basis for understanding the difference between equivalence and equality. The concepts of displacement and equivalence provide a new approach to understanding integers. African drumming becomes the context for an extensive unit on ratio and proportion. Teachers use inquiry-based teaching strategies that build on the concrete experiences of children. They act as coaches and guides to construct experiences that will help students find their own answers by asking increasingly sophisticated questions. Algebra Project students are encouraged to think about mathematics and to discuss and present their symbolic representations of important mathematical concepts. The Algebra Project also addresses professional standards by engaging students in the construction of mathematical concepts through a Five-Step curricular process that moves from familiar concrete experiences to abstract mathematics: participate in a physical event; make pictorial (graphic) representations or models of the event; discuss and write about the event in intuitive language(s); discuss and write about the event in structured language (identify key features); and develop symbolic representations for the key features of the event; make presentations to the class and apply these representations. The Algebra Project provides many opportunities for students to enhance their writing skills. The language arts component is well integrated within the curricular process. There are also opportunities to integrate the physical and chemical sciences around the ideas of benchmarks and displacements. The "feature talk" component of the project can help to enhance the understanding of identifying characteristics of the anatomy and physiology units in the sixth grade science curriculum.

The Algebra Project offers a three-stage training process that assists teachers in making transitions in their thinking and teaching styles. First, teachers experience the curriculum in much the way their students would, with an inquiry-based experiential curriculum and cooperative strategies for classroom management. Second, teachers are observed as they implement the curriculum, and are given feedback and guidance. This stage of training also includes follow-up seminars that expose teachers to additional curriculum, as well as providing them with more feedback and an opportunity to reflect on their experiences. Project sites must work with Algebra Project trainers and support staff in their region and the Algebra Project offices to develop strategies for Stage Two training and support that rely upon local resources to the greatest extent possible. Stage Three training is designed to support teachers' continuing development. It engages interested teachers in developing new curriculum units based on the experiential approach, or in further study into interdisciplinary areas that affect mathematics learning.

NATIONAL MULTICULTURAL INTERPRETER PROJECT

The National Multicultural Interpreter Project is supported by a five-year grant from the U.S. Department of Education Office of Rehabilitation Services Administration (RSA) at El Paso Community College. The project provides program assistance, as applicable, to the eleven other RSA Interpreter Training Projects, which provide interpreter education and training opportunities to all fifty states, as well as the District of Columbia, Puerto Rico, the Virgin Islands, Guam, and American Samoa.

The mission of the National Multicultural Interpreter Consortium is to improve the quantity and quality of interpreting services provided to individuals who are D-deaf, hard-of-hearing, and Deaf-Blind and from culturally diverse communities by providing educational opportunities, recruiting culturally diverse interpreters, and enhancing cultural sensitivity within the profession. The initial set of objectives included improved recruitment and retention of interpreters from culturally diverse backgrounds; development of multicultural interpreter curricula and materials; development of a multicultural curriculum; technical assistance to the national and regional RSA Interpreter Education Projects; workshops and training for interpreter educators; and the establishment of a National Multicultural Interpreter Consortium.

The following description is reprinted with permission from the NMIP Web site:

> A core multicultural curriculum and mode of instruction would enable students to (1) learn the history and contributions to society including the diverse D/deaf, hard of hearing, and Deaf-Blind and interpreter groups who comprise the population of the United States; (2) respect the culture and language of these diverse D/deaf and interpreter groups; (3) develop knowledge, understanding, and appreciation of one's own multiple group characteristics and how these characteristics can impart privilege or marginalize the individual or group; and (4) learn how to bring about social and structural equality and work toward that end. NMIP works for changes to many levels of activities within a program, including (1) exploring our own racial and ethnic identities including self-awareness activities for faculty, staff, and students; (2) building a community of learners by establishing program norms that include respect, inclusion, and trust; (3) expanding faculty and student perspectives by including new input from outside the mainstream or norm and validating the perspectives of all; (4) analyzing language and linguistic diversity issues by comparing and defining with ethnographic descriptive, not prescriptive tools; and (5) acknowledging and celebrating diversity and multicultural differences throughout the entire program.
>
> NMIP works specifically on what they call critically "invisible" and omitted cultural and ethnic issues. The first is invisibility—The significant omission of Deaf minority groups, Deaf women's issues, and other diversity issues in curriculum materials implies that these groups are of less value, importance, and significance in our society. The second issue is stereotyping—When a group is assigned traditional or rigid roles based on norms and standards of the dominant Deaf Culture in

instructional materials, activities, or interactions, students are denied a knowledge of the diversity and complexity of that group. Another invisible issue is selectivity—Textbooks, in particular, have perpetuated bias by offering only bilingual (ASL/English) or bicultural (Deaf/Hearing) interpretation of an issue, situation, or group of people; this restricts the knowledge, skill development, and real-life preparation of students in the field regarding varied perspectives of other culturally and linguistically diverse communities. Unreality, fragmentation, and linguistic bias are the last three areas of invisibility. Videotapes, general textbooks and other curriculum materials have presented an unrealistic portrayal of history, glossing over prejudice and discrimination. By separating issues relating to deaf minorities from the main body of text or curricular content, they imply that these issues by their fragmentation appear less important than issues of "mainstream" Deaf culture. And curriculum materials reflect the nature of the ASL and English as traditionally used by the white Deaf Community, which reflects cultural bias in the use of register, style, facial expressions, lexicon, and use of classifiers and gesture systems to represent cultural terms. This bias does not adequately represent the complexity and variation in ASL and English as used by Deaf people from culturally and linguistically diverse communities. It is significant to acknowledge that in many communities and educational programs, the diverse communities are now the "majority" minority.

NMIP believes that curriculum change is either superficial or it seeks to challenge the deep structures of the society's institutions to respond to the need to educate and empower the pluralistic society it serves. They use the terms of inclusion, infusion, and transformation to define the goals of their three approaches to curriculum change, which are adapted from Banks. Four levels refer to the depth of the curriculum change within the program.

A primary goal of NMIP's curriculum inclusion or improvement is to include the "omitted" or to correct the stereotyped portrayals of groups. A multicultural curriculum modification is accomplished either through curriculum inclusion or curriculum change. It is characterized by inclusion of the 3 C's of culture: cuisine, costumes, and crafts. This selective information is presented as a supplement, addendum, or in addition to what is currently taught. Multicultural content is "infused" into all aspects of the curriculum on a regular and routine basis; the information is about "all" people and presented to "all" students regardless of their racial, ethnic, or cultural background, and is woven into all courses and activities. It forms the basis for the faculty-student relationships with their communities. It can be seen in every unit, curriculum guide, book chosen, audiovisual aid chosen, and the physical environment of the program. It focuses on past problems and future potential, the patterns, issues, concepts, and trends that change over time. It is multiethnic, multicultural, interdisciplinary, and comparative in nature. Curriculum transformation and change goes beyond inclusion and infusion to a core value paradigm shift that leads to strong social action, equality, and transformative dimensions. In curriculum transformation and change the core principles and values of the status quo are challenged. At this level of transformation, all levels of the program are impacted, from the integration of the program into the community, the advisory boards, and faculty recruitment to curriculum materials, teaching methodology, and program activities.

NMIP uses the following questions as a guide for assessment:

- •◆ What are the underlying assumptions, principles, or norms of your program?
- •◆ What kinds of knowledge and skills are valued? What kinds of knowledge and skills are not valued?
- •◆ What changes do you envision making in your unit, module, course, or program?
- •◆ How will these assumptions, principles, and norms change as you include more materials and knowledge from previously excluded or "invisible" groups?
- •◆ How have multicultural seminars and readings changed your perspective of the profession?
- •◆ What human, media, or technical resources do you have or need to have access to?
- •◆ What types of changes in attitudes, knowledge, and skills as seen in behavior or skill demonstration do you hope to see in students taking your revised courses?

They provide the following list as an aid for getting started in rethinking a program and curriculum:

- •◆ Explore our unique multicultural American Deaf Communities to include race, ethnicity, gender, sexual orientation, religious, generational, age, geographical and regional, educational, political, economic and social class, and linguistic differences.
- •◆ Infuse diversity while promoting social justice and unity.
- •◆ Infuse multicultural concepts and activities across the curriculum.
- •◆ Organize the NMIP multicultural competencies and content across intercourse strategies:
- •◆ Provide general information on cultures: African American/ Black, American Indian/Alaskan Native, Asian/Pacific Islander, Euro-American/White, Hispanic/Latino in all courses: ASL

courses including fingerspelling, U.S. Deaf Community and culture courses, interpreting theory and skills development courses, internships and related courses.

•➤ Include multicultural readings in all units to discuss issues related to the profession in general.

•➤ Include multicultural writing and journal assignments related to issues.

•➤ Provide access to interaction and communication with individuals from culturally and linguistically diverse backgrounds as faculty, guest presenters, on videotapes, as mentors, and work experience supervisors in a wide variety of topics and areas not only confined to "multicultural topics."

•➤ Encourage the development of self-esteem with encouragement in self-exploration and pride for all racial, ethnic, cultural, and linguistic backgrounds.

•➤ Utilize appraisal and evaluation procedures that are unbiased. Consider portfolio approaches to provide alternative evaluation processes.

•➤ Encourage self-awareness and identity development in the context of a multicultural profession.

•➤ Provide opportunities for all students to develop leadership and communication skills in multicultural settings.

•➤ Provide opportunities to develop and emphasize the value and benefits of developing multicultural and multilingual skills in individuals and teams.

•➤ Determine culturally relevant norms and teach skills required or preferred by culturally diverse communities.

•➤ Provide all students access to develop computer literacy skills and internet skills so that they will be able to network and obtain a wide range of multicultural information.

FACING HISTORY AND OURSELVES

The following description is reprinted with permission from the Facing History and Ourselves Web site:

Founded in 1979, Facing History and Ourselves is a national nonprofit organization that offers educators an innovative, interdisciplinary approach to the teaching of citizenship. It is an approach that connects history to the day-to-day experiences of students by revealing the way violence and hate can destroy a society. The approach helps students discover that individuals can make a difference by examining how the decisions of ordinary people, little by little, shape an age and ultimately a history itself. Educators become familiar with Facing History's approach by experiencing it at workshops and institutes. There they encounter a model that helps students move from thought to judgment to participation by confronting the moral questions inherent in a rigorous examination of a particular history—the history of the decisions that undermined democracy in Weimar Germany and ultimately resulted in the Holocaust. It is a model that uses the methods of the humanities—inquiry, analysis, and interpretation—to help students examine the complexities of history and understand how the past relates to their own lives.

Facing History and Ourselves provides seminars, afternoon workshops, conferences, and adult education courses. Many teachers also meet individually with staff for individualized consultation in incorporating the Facing History approach into their instruction. In addition, Facing History's Resource Center provides educators nationwide with speakers and a lending library of relevant books, periodicals, and videos. Facing History keeps its programs timely and relevant through ongoing research on history and ethics. The staff has produced the resource books *Facing History and Ourselves: Holocaust and Human Behavior, Elements of Time,* and seven study guides: *Participating in Democracy: Choosing to Make a Difference, A Guide to the Film Schindler's List, Memphis: Building Community, A Guide to the American Experience, A Guide for the Rescuers of the Holocaust, A Guide to the New England Holocaust Memorial,* and *Survivors of the Holocaust.* A member of the National Diffusion Network, Facing History and Ourselves reaches nearly 900,000 students annually from its national headquarters in Boston and its regional offices in Chicago, Los Angeles, Memphis, New York, and San Francisco. The U.S. Department of Education has recognized Facing History as a exemplary program.

Facing History and Ourselves works based on the belief that education in a democracy must be what Alexis de Tocqueville called "an apprenticeship in liberty." Facing History helps students find meaning in the past and recognize the need for participation and responsible decision making. Students must know not only the triumphs of history, but also the failures, the tragedies, and the humiliations. Facing History believes that students must be trusted to examine history in all of its complexities, including its legacies of prejudice and discrimination, resilience and courage. This trust encourages young people to develop a voice in the conversations of their peer culture, as well as in the critical discussions and debates of their community and nation. For almost 25 years, Facing History has engaged teachers and students of diverse backgrounds in an examination of racism, prejudice, and anti-Semitism in order to promote the development of a more humane and informed citizenry. By studying the historical development of the Holocaust and other examples of collective violence, students make the essential connection between history and the moral choices they confront in their own lives. Facing History and Ourselves offers teachers and others in the community occasions to study the past, explore new ideas and approaches, and develop practical models for civic engagement that link history to the challenges of an increasingly interconnected world and the choices that young people make daily. Facing History students learn that apathy and indifference stifle hope. They discover how violence destroys families and nations. They seek opportunities to confront the isolation that fuels the misunderstandings, myths, and misinformation they have about the "other." Facing History helps students find answers to their questions. How can we prevent violence and end racism and anti-Semitism? How do we find the courage to protect human rights so that "never again" truly means that we have learned something by studying the events that led to one of the most violent times in the twentieth century?

THEATER OF THE OPPRESSED LABORATORY

The Theater of the Oppressed Laboratory, founded in New York City in July 1990, provides a forum for the practice, performance, and dissemination of the techniques of the Theater of the Oppressed, a form of popular education using interactive theater developed by Brazilian director and political activist Augusto Boal and others. The following description is reprinted with permission from the Theatre of the Oppressed Web site:

> TOPLAB is a group of educators, cultural and political activists, and artists whose work is based on extensive training and collaboration with Augusto Boal since its founding. TOPLAB conducts on-site training workshops on theater as an organizing tool for activists in neighborhood, labor, peace, human rights, youth, and community-based organizations. They work with educators, human service and mental health workers, union organizers, and community activists who are interested in using interactive theater as a tool for analyzing and exploring solutions to problems of oppression and power that arise in the workplace or school, and community problems connected to AIDS, substance abuse, family violence, homelessness, unemployment, racism, and sexism.
>
> Bridging the separation between actor (the one who acts) and

spectator (the one who observes but is not permitted to intervene in the theatrical situation), the Theater of the Oppressed is practiced by "spect-actors" who have the opportunity to both act and observe, and who engage in self-empowering processes of dialogue that help foster critical thinking. The theatrical act is thus experienced as conscious intervention, as a rehearsal for social action rooted in a collective analysis of shared problems of oppression. This particular type of interactive theater is rooted in the pedagogical and political principles specific to the popular education method developed by Brazilian educator Paulo Freire: (1) to see the situation lived by the participants; (2) to analyze the root causes of the situation; and (3) to act to change the situation following the precepts of social justice.

Just as the principal goal of popular education is to change the power relations in our society and to create mechanisms of collective power over all the structures of society, so too the principal goal of the Laboratory is to help groups explore and transform power relations of domination and subjugation that give rise to oppression. Within this learning process, (1) all participants are learners; (2) all participate in and contribute equally to the production of knowledge, which is a continuous dialogue; (3) the learners are the subject and not the object of the process; and (4) the objective of the process is to liberate participants from both internal and external oppression, so as to make them capable of changing their reality, their lives, and the society they live in. Since 1990, through the auspices of The Brecht Forum, the Laboratory has initiated and organized intensive workshops led by Augusto Boal in New York City. It has also planned and led more than two hundred public training workshops in the techniques of the Theater of the Oppressed. In this capacity, the Laboratory has brought together people from diverse backgrounds, occupations, and organizations, and functioned as a resource, information, and networking center serving individuals and groups interested in theater for social change.

The problem directly addressed by TOPLAB is one that underlies the very process of organizing for democratic social change: the relationship of means to end. The way people conceive of a specific problem—how they see themselves within it, how they interact with others who share similar oppressions, and how they organize (or do not organize) to propose and achieve solutions—is part of the problem itself. In other words, the nature of group process—specifically, the need to establish democratic group process as the means to achieving participatory democracy—needs to be addressed. One of the challenges of organizing, for example, is that marginalized people often lack confidence in their own thinking and ability to strategize, and therefore look to organizers for answers, and due to expediency, they may not find within the group the necessary support structures for developing strong leadership skills. Thus, despite meaningful victories the group may be able to achieve by following the lead of the organizer, this dynamic perpetuates long-term dependency and disempowerment. Therefore, just as the principal goal of popular education is to change the power relations in our society and to create mechanisms of collective power over the structures of society, so too the principal goal of the Theater of the Oppressed Laboratory is to help groups, within the context of a democratic learning process, to confront and transform power relations of domination and subjugation that give rise to oppression. The Laboratory has given workshops in the New York City public schools, and at colleges and universities in New York and elsewhere, and has developed and conducted on-site workshops with different community organizations to explore problems specific to their particular work: the role of the arts in the struggle against racism, at the North Star Conference; building solidarity among women, at the Urban Pathways/Travelers Hotel Women's Shelter; AIDS prevention, with the Shaman Theater-Pregones-ASPIRA coalition; and promoting health among homeless people with HIV/AIDS, at the Foundation for Research on Sexually Transmitted Diseases. The Laboratory also led a workshop at the April 1995 teach-in in New York, "Out from under the Bell Curve: A Teach-in on Confronting Right-wing Ideology and Social Policy," and presents workshops each year at the annual Socialist Scholars Conference held in New York City. Members of the Laboratory attended the International Festivals of the Theater of the Oppressed held in France in 1991 and in Rio de Janeiro in 1993, strengthening relations with theater activists from twenty-two different countries, while planning the creation of an International Association of the Theater of the Oppressed. The Theater of the Oppressed Laboratory has presented workshops in indigenous communities of the Los Altos and Las Canadas regions of the Mexican state of Chiapas, and worked with the Diocese of San Cristobal de las Casas in the cities of Comitan and San Cristobal, offering training workshops for social justice workers and educators. Other work in Mexico included training peace and social activists who were part of a youth community in the state of Tabasco, and with street children in Mexico City, and peace and solidarity groups based in the capital. TOPLAB was also a participant in the International Festival of Alternative Theater (Reunion Internacional de Especialistas en Teatro Alternativa), held in Mexico City in 1997. TOPLAB has presented workshops in El Quiche, Guatemala, in conjunction with Caritas for health and literacy educators, women's rights groups, and community organizers, and in an alcoholism treatment center, working with both clients and recovery professionals, and presented a staff-development workshop in Guatemala City for psychologists and teachers of at-risk pupils. In addition to targeted training workshops, TOPLAB members have worked in various street theater projects around the themes of globalization, neoliberalism, and international solidarity, and to protest United States aggression in Iraq and the Balkans.

The Laboratory also gives advice and support to individuals and groups who use the techniques of the Theater of the Oppressed in their particular field (education, social work, community organizing, the arts). The Images Theater Collective, for instance, grew out of the meetings and study sessions led by the Laboratory on the political potential of interactive theater. In 1992, as part of the movement to counter the official Columbus Quincentennial celebrations, the Collective wrote and performed a play, based on Image Theater techniques, on colonial oppression and resistance in Latin America. In addition, as a result of Laboratory activity, Theater of the Oppressed theory and techniques have been integrated into the basic curriculum of both the Puerto Rican Traveling Theatre Training Unit and the Education Program of the Latino Experimental Fantastic Theater. Finally, in 1993, the Laboratory became an independent affiliate of the Institute for Popular Education at The Brecht Forum.

TWO-WAY IMMERSION BILINGUAL EDUCATION AT MADAWASKA ELEMENTARY SCHOOL AND GATEWAY ELEMENTARY SCHOOL, L'ACADIEN DU HAUT ST-JEAN

This Two-Way Bilingual Education Immersion Program is a K-5 French/English program that will eventually go through grade 8. The project is a consortium of two school districts of the St. John Valley, which borders French New Brunswick, Canada. It is an additive bilingual program, meaning that all students learn a second language without compromising their first language. This is the only program of its kind in the state of Maine. Between the two school districts, there are eight bilingual classes involving a total of about 300 students, representing one-third of the student population of one district, and one-half of the student population of the other. During the summer, the program also sponsors a French immersion camp for students grades K-6.

The following description is adapted with permission from Mary Lunney, "Two-Way French Immersion in Rural Maine," *ACIE Newsletter* 5, no. 1: 4–5:

Students in L'Acadien du Haut St-Jean develop fluency and literacy in two languages (French and English), achieve proficiency in all academic subjects while meeting or exceeding district standards, cultivate an understanding and appreciation of other cultures, and develop positive attitudes toward fellow students, their families and their community. Emphasis on French instruction in the early grades allows English-speakers ample exposure to the target language: French. French-speakers have the opportunity to expand their vocabulary and build a strong base in their first language, enabling them to be more successful as they begin to acquire English orally, and later as they transfer reading and writing skills into English. Emphasis on English increases after fourth grade.

Two-way bilingual education immersion is a rigorous academic program in which French and English are used as the vehicle of instruction and not taught simply as a subject. Thematic units integrate the curriculum, making the languages more meaningful to the students, and providing them with enough exposure to practice, use, and extend their vocabulary. Teachers engage students in active participatory activities requiring responses in the language of instruction, be it the native or second language for the student. Hands-on classroom projects provide additional opportunities for students to use their second language. Teachers use a reciprocal-interactive approach and cooperative learning techniques to encourage students to interact with one another in their second language. Students who are native speakers of French and of English are together in the same class. They are instructed in either French or English. The languages are always kept separate for instruction.

Teachers do not use translation for comprehension. Instead, they use a multitude of second language acquisition techniques to make language and content understandable for all students. Students are provided with opportunities to assist and learn from one another, allowing second language acquisition to occur naturally. Teachers establish an environment where students must use the target language to meet real-life needs. This approach develops language skills through hands-on classroom experiences. Students more readily attach vocabulary to an activity in a hands-on or experiential setting.

All two-way language immersion instructors are bilingual teachers with native-like fluency in French/English. Resource teachers and instructional aides also provide support. Teachers serve on the district's Curriculum Design Team to ensure alignment of the curriculum to what is mandated by the district. Ongoing training for all staff is provided by office personnel, outside trainers, and by the district's staff development team. Staff participates in courses, workshops, and on-site visits to other immersion programs. A custom-designed class in ESL is offered— through distance learning—by the University of Southern Maine. Summer institutes are offered with the collaboration of the New Brunswick French immersion teachers or through the University of Maine. Parental involvement is an integral part of the L'Acadien du Haut St-Jean program. It is not only a bilingual school, but calls itself a bilingual community. Parents are encouraged to volunteer in the classroom and to work with their children on language skills at home. Workshops help parents become knowledgeable about the second-language process and to teach them how to support a child's second-language abilities as they increase. The Parent Advisory Committee (PAC) offers opportunities for parents to contribute to the school program. Planning cultural events, working on fundraisers, and providing information are just a few of the ways that the PAC supports the school. A regular output of news releases and other newspaper articles has allowed the community ample opportunities to become aware of the program goals and activities.

The Saint John Valley certainly seems like a bilingual society because people constantly switch back and forth between French and English, often within one sentence. But most Valley school-age kids in Maine now consider English their first language, and French speakers have become the minority in the Valley's public schools. The New Brunswick side of the Valley is largely the opposite. A generation ago, most children in the St. John Valley entered the school speaking French. Geographical isolation provided a protective barrier for French speakers in the Valley. Then the English-only policy was introduced in the schools, as the outside world encroached through radio and TV; it was like a cultural crowbar that ripped holes in the wall. Students were encouraged to learn English as quickly as possible, even if that meant losing their native language. A 1959 teachers' handbook put out by the Madawaska Teachers Club opened with a stern warning that teachers should ensure that English was spoken at all times. "Any teacher violates her trust when she encourages children to speak anything but English at recess, around the playground, before or after school or even away from school," the handbook states. Some teachers went so far as to anglicize their students' names. Clayton Belanger, superintendent of School Administrative District 24 in the Van Buren area, remembers getting caught speaking French at recess when he was a child in a nearby district. The nuns who taught in the public school hit him with a strap. He grew up believing that French was an inferior language. "If someone was English, they definitely were superior," Belanger says. Even in sports, he says, "they were going to beat us because they were English." A 1992 study by a professor from the University of Moncton, New Brunswick, found that children in the St. John Valley were rapidly assimilating, losing both their knowledge of the French language and their Acadian identity. "That was like an alarm to us," says Marc Chasse of Fort Kent. Chasse and others formed the Club Francais, which distributes French dictionaries and storybooks and sponsors a French-speaking contest in local high schools. Club members have supported French masses at a Madawaska church. Other efforts got under way to revive interest in the Acadian culture. Residents successfully lobbied Congress in 1990 to set up and fund the Maine Acadian Cultural Preservation Commission. A group began restoring a landmark Catholic church in the village of Lille into a cultural center. The annual Acadian Festival in Madawaska now draws as many as 5,000 people.

> Consistent with efforts to revive French, two classrooms (one in northern Maine and the other in Quebec City) were among more than 100 classes that participated in partner-class projects through their involvement with the Orillas Multilingual Computer Network. Both classes were composed of upper-elementary-grade schoolchildren. The class in northern Maine was composed of English-speaking students from a Francophone background. Their teacher was interested in his pupils recovering the cultural and linguistic heritage of their parents and grandparents through contact with French speakers in Quebec. The classes exchanged "mystery cultural packages" containing soil samples, photos, examples of local flora and fauna, and individual and class photographs. They also worked on a journalism project that resulted in a bilingual magazine at year's end. (Cummins and Sayers 1995)

The Two Way program was initiated in 1995, catering largely to children of Acadian heritage who had either French or English as their native language. The St. John Valley districts received a federal grant from Title VII for $1.18 million to pay for teacher training, materials, and administrative costs between 1995 and 2000. At the outset, there was some trepidation on the part of the staff, parents, and administrators. Teachers worried that they weren't qualified to teach in French, and they could lose their jobs if they refused. Although some parents embraced the program, others feared that it would interfere with other programs in their schools, such as popular multigrade classes in Frenchville. Parents also questioned whether their children could handle learning two different languages at once. Administrators acknowledged that it might be hard to find teachers as the program expanded to higher grade levels, where teaching would involve more sophisticated vocabulary. Some educators worried that the program would attract only the best students, since some parents were reluctant to enroll children already struggling in school. However, the bilingual program ultimately won enthusiastic backing. The program reinforces "what I wanted to do in the first place, but I didn't have the support to do," claims a parent who wants her children to maintain French. A school board member says the program is helping to change community attitudes toward the French language. "We've been brought up for a long time to see French as a street language, and not worthy to be taught," he says. "We never learned to read and write it. . . . It was not important enough to have in school. . . . We're seeing a big change in that now. Kids, they just love singing French songs. They just love speaking French. It's like it's become a new fad." The program wants to keep expanding opportunities for bilingualism. An application has been submitted to extend the project into high school and pre-kindergarten, which are areas not served by the present project. In addition, monies have been available to l'Acadien sixth and seventh graders who want to participate in summer immersion courses in Canada.

TEACHING ABOUT WHITENESS

Gregory Jay, professor of English at the University of Wisconsin in Milwaukee, responds to several concerns raised by some versions of multiculturalism: the questions of race should not be a focus only in discussing people of color, during add-on curricula for "Black History Month" or "Japanese American Week." According to Jay, "silence about whiteness lets everyone continue to harbor prejudices and misconceptions; whiteness has been a significant legal and political category, and thus requires examination; and whiteness has been a significant aesthetic and cultural value (or symbol or commodity), and thus requires interpretation." He further points out that teaching about whiteness helps move classes beyond the "celebrate diversity" model of multiculturalism; whiteness pedagogy moves antiracist education in new directions by presenting difficult challenges to the very idea of "race." Also, he says, studying whiteness can change the social dynamics of any classroom community, whatever its ethno-racial composition.

The following discussion questions have been reprinted with permission from Gregory Jay's Teaching about Whiteness Web site:

- Are "white" people a "race"?
- Is "white" a term for a racial group or a cultural group? Is there any such thing as "white" culture? Are all its practitioners of the same skin color?

•• When did the idea of "white" people get invented? Whose idea was it? Who was originally included in the idea of a "white" people? Who has been included since?

•• What makes "white" people "white"? Skin color? Hair? Nose? Language? Culture? Politics?

•• Are "white" people the same as "Caucasians"? "Aryans"? "Anglo-Saxons"? When did each of these terms first come into use? How do they differ?

•• Are Jews "white" people? What about other "white" ethnics, such as Italians or Spaniards?

•• How do Asian Americans differ from "white" people? Appearance? Culture? Legal standing?

•• How "white" do you have to be to be "white"? If an African American can "pass," is that person "white"? If a "white" person has African American ancestors, is that person "white" or "black"? If an African American person has European ancestors, is that person "black" or "white"? Can you be "part white" or "part black" in America?

•• Are there "whiter whites" and "blacker blacks"? Is color discrimination something that only happens between races, or within ethno-racial groups as well?

•• Should "white" people celebrate their ethno-racial heritage just like other groups? (White History Month?)

•• Does talking about "whiteness" help the fight against racism, or just become one more way of not talking about African Americans and other people of color?

•• Is "white" a "panethnic" category along the lines of "Asian American" or "African American" or "American Indian"? Or should we speak of "European Americans," even though not all of them are "white"?

•• If "white" is not a coherent cultural or ethnic category, what kind of category is it? Social? Economic? Political?

Jay also recommends several types of classroom projects and inquiries:

•• Keyword Exercises: Have students collect the entries on "race," "white," "Caucasian," "Aryan," "black," and "Negro" (for example) from at least two dictionaries and two encyclopedias. Compare the results, and then ask students to try writing their own definitions of some of these terms. Or have them use an interview technique, in which they record definitions of these terms gathered by interviewing other students, family members, teachers, librarians, etc.

•• Historical Research: Have students find uses of the word "white" and "black" (or "colored" or "Negro") in legal or political documents, such as acts of Congress, Supreme Court rulings, state and local statutes, etc. Discuss "whiteness" as a legal category (or legal fiction).

➡ Life Analysis: Have students make a list of ten things they normally do during the week. Then have them imagine that they woke up one day to find that their "race" had changed to [fill in the blank]. Going through their lists, students should analyze how each thing might be different for them were their "race" different. Would they be able to go to such places, talk to such people, enjoy such events, etc.? Would they feel comfortable doing so? What would be the chances that people of that race would be found doing these things in these places in these ways? What other things might they be doing instead? What real differences, in other words, does "race" make each day in our lives?

➡ Media analysis: Look for images of whiteness in the media. What kinds and types of whiteness appear most often? Are there different classes of white people? If so, how are they represented differently by the media? How long can one watch television or read a newspaper or magazine without encountering anything but white people, or mostly white people? Have students bring in copies of major newspapers and magazines and analyze the distribution of images of whiteness and blackness. Make a list of the top grossing films of the last five years and consider whether their characters and presumed audience show a bias toward whiteness.

➡ Literary analysis: Read portions of Toni Morrison's *Playing in the Dark: Whiteness and the Literary Imagination.* Using texts by white authors, analyze the way whiteness gets constructed through comparisons to a dark or black "other." Debate whether or not schools should offer courses with names such as "Major White American Authors" or "The White Tradition in American Literature." Compare texts by white and black authors to analyze what difference whiteness makes (for example, compare Franklin's *Autobiography* with Douglass's *Narrative,* or the poems of Langston Hughes with those of Robert Frost, or the stories of Alice Walker with those of William Faulkner). Have students rewrite particular stories or passages by changing the race of the narrator or main character.

THE IMPORTANCE OF LEADERSHIP

The Institute for Community Integration identified four secondary schools through a national advisory panel; each school was studied to understand how these schools achieved exemplary results for students both with and without disabilities. The intent of the "Beacons of Excellence" project was to identify factors associated with schools whose students with disabilities were achieving exemplary learning results within the context of all students achieving such results. Included in their study were the High School of Telecommunication Arts and Technology in Brooklyn, New York, Fred J. Page High School in Franklin, Tennessee, William H. Turner Technical Arts High School in Miami, Florida, and Sinagua High School in Flagstaff, Arizona. What the Institute found was that Leadership emerged as a key factor in successful inclusive education across each of the exemplary programs studied. Key factors of leadership included challenging all students and teachers to high standards, building an inclusive and collaborative learning community, fostering a school culture of innovation and creativity, engaging stakeholders in school leadership, promoting professional development, hiring staff who reinforce the school's values and mission, and using data for decision making and school improvement planning. Such lists of leadership factors have appeared in many contexts. But it is important to note that this research concluded successful inclusive education rests on a style of leadership that promotes inclusive community involvement in the school leadership and decision-making processes.

FINAL COMMENTS

Multiculturalism has become an enormous "market area" for materials, consulting, staff development, and leadership training. There is an overwhelming number of resources, organizations offering assistance, and agencies seeking substantial remuneration for services that promote multicultural education and organizational diversity. A quick use of any search engine on the Internet using the keywords "multicultural" and "diversity education" will elicit thousands of Web pages of links and programs, as well as hundreds of promotions for services or publications. This book attempts to introduce key ideas that can help the reader sift through the deluge of resources and identify those that make the most sense for his or her particular context and immediate goals. Toward this end, this chapter has highlighted a range of case studies that can help the reader consider the kinds of options for which he or she might seek further resources. Chapter 7 of this book provides a current directory of associations and organizations that promote multicultural education. Chapter 8 offers a selected and annotated list of print resources, along with Internet and other nonprint resources.

Most available materials and diversity training programs do not necessarily reflect recent considerations of critical multiculturalism, so it behooves an educator to carefully analyze "exemplary programs" and award-winning or well-funded nonprofit organizations for what these associations and opportunities offer. In many cases, multicultural materials can be modified to avoid reifying cultures or perpetuating a simplistic "celebration of diversity" approach. Attention to the ways in which cultures can be understood as emerging and changing, multiple in their own identities, and overlapping in their "borders" can often enrich an initially weak unit plan or diversity strategy. Ongoing assessment that includes multiple constituencies as equal partners in decision making contributes significantly to the democratic nature of diversity education and is an excellent model for the working of a multicultural, democratic community in itself.

REFERENCES AND FURTHER READING

Algebra Project Web site: *http://www.algebra.org.*

Cornelius, Carol. 1999. *Iroquois Corn in a Culture-Based Curriculum: A Framework for Respectfully Teaching about Cultures.* Albany, NY: State University of New York Press.

Cummins, Jim, and Sayers, Dennis. 1995. *Brave New Schools: Challenging Cultural Illiteracy through Global Learning Networks.* New York: St. Martin's.

Facing History and Ourselves Web site: *http://www.facing.org/facing/fhao2.nsf.*

Institute on Community Integration, Beacons of Excellence Web site: *http://ici2. umn.edu/beacons/overview/default.html.*

Intergeneration Orchestra of Omaha Web site: *http://www.public.iastate.edu/~manderso/igo/index.html.*

Jay, Gregory. "Teaching about Whiteness" Web site: *http://www.uwm.edu/~gjay/ Whiteness/Teachwhiteness.html.*

Lunney, Mary. "Two-Way French Immersion in Rural Maine." *ACIE Newsletter* 5, no. 1: 4–5.

Media Awareness Network Web site: *http://www.media-awareness.ca/eng/ issues/minrep/resource/teachunt.htm.*

Moses, Robert P. 1994. "Remarks on the Struggle for Citizenship and Math/ Sciences Literacy." *Journal of Mathematical Behavior* 13: 107–111.

National Multicultural Interpreter Project Web site: *http://www.epcc.edu/ Community/NMIP/welcome.html.*

Ross, Andrew. 1994. *The Chicago Gangster Theory of Life: Nature's Debt to Society.* New York: Verso.

Theater of the Oppressed Laboratory Web site: *http://www.toplab.org/.*

Weaver, John, and Karen Grindall. 1998. "Surfing and Getting Wired in a Fifth Grade Classroom: Critical Pedagogical Methods and Techno-Culture." In *Unauthorized Methods: Strategies for Critical Teaching,* Joe Kincheloe and Shirley Steinberg, eds., 231–251. New York: Routledge.

Chapter Five

❧ Political and Legal Issues

This chapter introduces the political and legal issues of multicultural and diversity education through five main sections. First we examine theoretical issues in the politics of multiculturalism, and the connections between diversity, identity, and citizenship education. The bulk of this chapter concerns state and local frameworks and educational standards documents for the legal support they offer and require. The chapter then examines the relationship between the standards documents and high-stakes testing. The role of unions in the politics of education is discussed. Finally, challenges to multiculturalism and diversity education need to be understood as political opportunities that face educators committed to the ideas and curricular practices outlined in this volume.

DIVERSITY, IDENTITY, AND CITIZENSHIP

Carlos Alberto Torres writes, "The connections between democracy and multiculturalism are among the most contested polemics of our time" (Torres 1999, 42). He quotes Cornel West:

> The new cultural politics of difference are neither simply oppositional in contesting the mainstream (or *male*stream) for inclusion nor transgressive in the avant-gardist sense of shocking conventional bourgeois audiences. Rather they are distinct articulations of talented (and usually privileged) contributors to culture who desire to align themselves with demoralized, demobilized, depoliticized, and disorganized people in order to empower and enable social action and, if possible, to enlist collective insurgency for the expansion of freedom, democracy, and individuality. (West 1993, 11–12)

In citing West, Torres asserts that multiculturalism in any form, shape, or color relates to the politics of difference and the emerging social struggles over racialized, gendered, and classist societies. Torres suggests discussions on multiculturalism in the United States should start with a subtle but important differentiation among notions of multiculturalism as a social movement and as a theoretical approach, multicultural education as a reform movement, and citizenship education as a curriculum-oriented specialty. Given the particular characteristics of U.S. racial dynamics, Torres believes citizenship education should take into account issues of racial identity and cultural diversity in working toward a conception of citizenship-building as a specifically anti-racist pedagogy.

Multiculturalism as a broad social movement tackles issues of race, gender, ethnicity, sexual orientation, class, and other relations of "difference" in society at large. As a philosophical, theoretical, and political orientation, multiculturalism goes beyond school reform. In the United States, multicultural education has been dominated by a particularly narrow range of political, theoretical, and cultural perspectives on diversity, often named "liberal multiculturalism." Proponents of liberal multiculturalism argue that this broad social movement makes two big promises: (1) multiculturalism will increase fairness (by representing the range and richness of America's different ethnicities); and (2) multiculturalism will increase tolerance by exposing students to multiple perspectives on the meaning of history. Critics note that this view of multiculturalism pluralizes the notion of an American identity by insisting on attention to a range of ethnic and racial groups; they also point out that this form of multiculturalism freezes in place "a unified concept of identity."

Identity, though, is more complicated than this, and is more multifaceted. It cannot be understood in these simple terms. People live multiple identities; group identities are formed in varying historical and cultural contexts; and so on. This is why many people who work in the field of multicultural and diversity education use the term "diversity." Diversity specifically refers to the plurality of identities, and it is seen as a condition of human existence rather than as the effect of an enunciation of differences that constitute hierarchies and asymmetries of power (Macedo and Bartolomé 2000; Scott, 1989). Identities are constructed in processes of contestation and struggle, and in practices of solidarity and cultural experience; they are based on perceptions of knowledge, experience, and power. They are also, themselves, processes of learning that are context-dependent and open to interpretation (Torres 1999).

As a reform movement, multicultural education shares much of its history with the movements of suffrage, civil rights, freedom of speech, and affirmative action. In one sense, each has contributed to our understanding of diversity as a central component of citizenship in the United States. Together, they suggest a natural link between equality of political opportunity and equality of social opportunity. A central role of education was once framed by Paulo Freire: What role, if any, should educational institutions and practices play in the constitution of the social pact that articulates democracy? The question places education as a reform movement at the center of serious political debates regarding the establishment and ongoing development of a democratic culture. Within these debates we find all sorts of philosophical and cultural conflicts about how people construct or enable the growth of a "democratic citizen." A political conflict of interests emerges in these debates: democracy implies a process of participation where all are considered equal; but education involves a process through which young people are brought to identify with the principles and forms of life of the "mature" members of society (Donald 1992).

Multicultural education as citizenship education is therefore a process of cultural nurturing. It is *also* a process of articulating principles—principles of pedagogic and democratic socialization *in* individuals who are neither "blank slates" in cognitive or ethical terms, nor fully equipped for the exercise of their democratic rights and obligations. This central problem of education—how to contribute to the democratic pact—is confounded by the complexities that teachers face as they relate to the demands of a common public school increasingly segregated by race and class, in a society with a growing gap between the haves and have-nots, where gender distinctions continue to be central to school discrimination, and in cultural contexts that deny the legitimacy of other categories of difference. This is the context in which policymakers, teachers, researchers, and other citizens call forth the goals of diversity and multiculturalism.

It is important to note that citizenship may be defined in terms of civic virtues or legal status. Civic virtues point to a sense of solidarity that unites individuals around common goals. These goals include, at the very least, how to survive and live together in our diverse society. However, these goals can also be accomplished through a more ambitious agenda: how to thrive as a community of communities, as a culture of cultures, drawing from our cultural diversity as a cultural strength, and as a useful tenet of policy. Yet, as Todd Gitlin (1995) cautions us, "The question is how to cultivate the spirit of solidarity across the lines of difference—solidarity with 'anyone who suffers.' For surely that spirit cannot be expected to generate spontaneously inside fortified groups, each preoccupied with refining its differences from other groups" (217). We need to develop flexible frameworks for solidarity in schools that take seriously the need for democratic reform. Cultural diversity is a major by-product of the growing process of economic, cultural, and political globalization, a conglomeration of processes that has no parallel in the history of humankind. Globalization has produced all sorts of implications for the multicultural, multilingual, and multiethnic configurations of local communities in the United States and elsewhere.

Yet in the current climate of high-stakes testing, educators question a focus on multiculturalism and diversity. "We did that back in the '80s," caricatures a special report by the Rethinking Schools organization (2000, 3). Educators can point to a number of minimally effective changes that have become part of most school programs since Martin Luther King Day celebrations became standard elements of the calendar, textbooks have been purchased with multicultural issues in mind, staff in-service workshops have become routine, and the public display of blatantly offensive attitudes has become inappropriate. Multiculturalism has been cartooned by the political right as divisive, Balkanizing, "politically correct," ethnic cheerleading. Such criticisms have been accompanied by broader attacks on people of color and people who are poor. Rethinking Schools lists, for example, the repeal of affirmative action, skyrocketing incarceration rates (especially of black men), families kicked off welfare with no other supports in place, increasing homeless populations, and jingoistic anti-immigrant initiatives.

High-stakes testing requires that every single thing that happens in the school be targeted toward increasing students' scores. One might argue that there is little time for multiculturalism when preparation for the tests is so essential. Nevertheless, an educator can argue that multicultural and diversity programs will easily save money in the long run by working to make sure that the school community is successful for *all* students (for example, early initiatives in elementary grades can reduce costs of remedial education, violence-reduction initiatives, and other special programs in later grades). A careful study of the tests on which students must perform well, ironically, can often lead to "legal" or "political" support for changes and innovations in the curriculum.

STATE AND NATIONAL FRAMEWORKS AND STANDARDS

On the one hand, the recommendations and legal expectations of professional associations, state and provincial governments, union policy documents, and other sources of frameworks and standards should be a resource for the implementation of multicultural and diversity education. On the other hand, they may be vague, inconsistent, or silent on issues of diversity. A quick trip to the Web page of your favorite association or state or local department of education should provide an initial glimpse of what is available. In some cases, these documents provide legal guidance and support for diversity education. In other cases, you can use the standards as justification for educational policies or practices that are part of your diversity agenda.

By far the most common location of multicultural and diversity standards for curricula is within the areas of social studies and citizenship education. Most states and school districts include attention to diversity in the curriculum and articulate a number of goals for understanding and appreciating the variety of histories and cultures represented in a pluralist society. Often, the standards and frameworks suggest a simplistic "add-on" approach to the curriculum. We must remember that these are minimum expectations that in no way restrict multicultural and diversity goals, but rather provide a starting point for policy and planning. An event, course, strand of the curriculum, or organizational policy need not be tied merely to the goal of one standard, but may address several at one time, or, indeed, may address some standards while also going beyond these standards in implementing more sophisticated goals.

Social Studies and Citizenship Education

The state of New Jersey begins its list of standards for social studies by declaring that this area of the curriculum "must promote civic and democratic principles so that students become informed and active citizens." Performance indicators include a range of social action experiences, from understanding the rights and responsibilities of all citizens based on the U.S. Constitution to locating, analyzing, organizing, and applying information about public issues and recognizing multiple points of view. These goals, along with "promoting the general welfare of the community," would suggest particular attention to the diversity of one's community, the value of multiple perspectives on social issues within that community, and serious participation in the public discussion of that community.

The standards also include important references to the use of literature, history, the arts, and humanities to analyze, understand, compare, and contrast cultural expression from different historical and social settings. "Comparing and contrasting divergent interpretations of historical turning points using available evidence" is a key feature of these standards. Through the study of different political systems, with special attention to democracy, the history of relations among different political groups and entities, the history of warfare, and the history of political leadership, students are expected to "synthesize historical facts and interpretations to reach personal conclusions about significant historical events," and to "analyze and formulate policy statements demonstrating an understanding of issues, standards, and conflicts related to universal human rights." By the end of eighth grade, students should be prepared to:

> compare and contrast developments in societies separated by time and/or distance; compare and contrast fixed customs of societies in the past and the present, and explain how these customs represent the society's beliefs; understand how family, community, and social institutions function to meet individual and group needs; and understand how historical and contemporary ideas, perceptions, and occurrences have led to prejudice, discrimination, expulsion, genocide, slavery, and the Holocaust. [By the end of twelfth grade, students should be prepared to] evaluate the views, beliefs, and impact of different social groups on a given historical event or issue; evaluate how individuals, groups, and institutions influence society's problems; analyze historical and contemporary circumstances in which institutions function either to maintain continuity or to promote change; argue an ethical position regarding a dilemma from the study of turning points in history; and evaluate actions an individual, group, or institution might take to counteract incidents of prejudice, discrimination, expulsion, genocide, slavery, and the Holocaust. (New Jersey Department of Education Web site)

This does not even include the standards regarding the study of varying cultures and economic forces, ideas, and institutions, throughout the history of the state, the country, and the world, each of which are included with separate "progress indicators." Surely any idea for multicultural education that an educator has in the state of New Jersey could be justified as an attempt to address some collection of the standards for the curriculum in social studies.

In the state of Wyoming, benchmarks for culture/cultural diversity include having students explain how various cultural influences impact society; students are expected to communicate how personal identity is shaped by and impacts culture, groups, institutions, and world events. Students in Oregon must experience a common curriculum that includes understanding relationships among events, issues, and developments in different spheres of human activity (i.e., economic, social, political, cultural); identify and analyze diverse perspectives on and historical interpretation of issues and events; and understand and interpret events, issues, and developments within and across eras of world history.

In Arizona, students in first through third grades should know and be able to do the following: describe the various backgrounds of people living in the United States and the ways they have become members of one nation (with emphasis on shared principles, goals, customs, and traditions; the diversity of one's school and community and the benefits and challenges of a diverse population); identify and describe the symbols, icons, songs, and traditions of the United States that exemplify ideals and provide continuity and a sense of community across time; describe the rights and responsibilities of citizenship; and describe the basic structure and concepts of the U.S. government. Students in high school must be able to explain the philosophical foundations of the U.S. political system in terms of the inalienable rights and the purpose of government, analyze historical sources and ideals of the structure of that government, and understand the U.S. Constitution from the perspective of its framers. Important cultural stories are expected to be part of the curriculum, and American heroes are to be understood as including those who fought for the rights and freedoms of others (including Chief Joseph, Chief Manuelito, Abraham Lincoln, Harriet Tubman, Martin Luther King, Jr., and Cesar Chávez); students should be able to describe the legacy and cultures of prehistoric America as well as Spanish and Mexican colonization as part of Arizona history, include a world history perspective on the social studies, and develop historical interpretations of the complexity of cause and effect in the context in which ideas and past events unfold.

Kentucky also includes performance descriptions. In the category of culture and society, middle-school students should demonstrate an understanding of the common elements of various cultures and the unique perspectives that develop as different cultures address their human needs in similar and different ways; students must also be able to make reasonable decisions, address issues, explain concepts, and/or solve problems using fully developed examples. Skills they are expected to demonstrate include, but are not limited to, reading, interpreting, and evaluating information; making comparisons; identifying multiple causes and effects; drawing conclusions and justifying explanations; considering multiple solutions and making decisions by applying criteria; and discriminating among plausible answers. All of the above are examples of the sorts of standards and frameworks that can be used to support or legitimate curricular goals in multicultural and diversity education.

In British Columbia, social responsibility is grouped into a number of sections, including, for example, the solving of problems in peaceful ways, valuing diversity and defending human rights, and exercising democratic rights and responsibilities. In some other provinces of Canada, such as Ontario, social studies is noted to include the study of current events; such study "forms an integral component of the social studies, history, and geography curriculum, enhancing both the relevance and the immediacy of the program. Discussion of current events not only creates student interest, but helps students understand their world and the relationship between past events and present-day situations. The study of current events needs to be thought of not as a separate topic removed from the program but as both included in and extending the expectations found in the curriculum. (Ontario Ministry of Education Web site).

In Vermont, the personal development standards include such areas as interactions ("students interact respectfully with others, including those with whom they have differences"), conflict resolution ("students use systematic and collaborative problem-solving processes, including mediation, to negotiate and resolve conflicts"), and roles and responsibilities ("students analyze their roles and responsibilities in their family, their school, and their community"); civic/social responsibility standards include two for human diversity: cultural expression ("students demonstrate understanding of the cultural expressions that are characteristic of particular groups") and effects of prejudice ("students demonstrate understanding of the concept of prejudice, and of its effects on various groups") (Vermont Department of Education Web site).

These types of goals are broader in their multicultural efforts, perhaps, than some of the very specific content standards that some states and provinces have adopted. But even in those areas of the United States and Canada where the content standards seem to be fairly narrow in their attempts to codify student performance expectations, there is always an official effort made to promote the social studies, civics education, social responsibility, or government and economics as essential to democratic participation in a pluralist society. The important thing to remember is that these documents are legal grounds for the explanation and justification of your multicultural and diversity efforts. If in doubt about where to find the specific standard your program addresses, consider a review of the introductory comments at the head of the document. For example, the Louisiana Department of Education social studies content standards introduction to the section on civics (citizenship and government) incorporates strong general support for diversity education across the curriculum:

> In order for citizens to exercise their rights and fulfill their responsibili-
> ties as members of a self-governing society, they must acquire the
> knowledge and skills necessary for informed, responsible participation
> in political life. A commitment to the fundamental principles of Ameri-
> can constitutional democracy is essential to its preservation and pro-
> gression. Because a democratic society must rely on the knowledge,
> skills, and virtues of its citizens, the study of civics is central to the pur-
> pose of American education. The standards and benchmarks contained
> in this strand should be applied throughout the social studies curricu-
> lum. (Louisiana Department of Education Web site)

If the standards do not directly suggest multicultural or diversity
themes, then they can often be used to argue for multiculturalism. For
example, the California history–social studies content standards outline
as the first standard for kindergarten through fifth grade, "Historical empathy for how people lived and worked long ago reinforces the concept
of civic behavior: how we interact respectfully with each other, following
rules and respecting the rights of others" (California Department of Education Web site). In Colorado's model content standards, "Citizenship
skills are required for competent participation in the political process.
These include the capacity to influence policies and decisions by working with others, clearly articulating interests and making them known to
key decision and policy makers, building coalitions, negotiating, compromising, seeking consensus, and managing conflicts" (Colorado Department of Education Web site). Such standards could be used to work
in favor of or against diversity; this sort of ambiguity of standards is
common because of the politics of creating these documents and then
obtaining legal status. Educators working to achieve multicultural and
diversity education can easily use them to support their efforts. To claim
interpretation proactively is one successful political strategy.

Other Curricular Areas

Outside of social studies and civics, one can find serious attention to
multicultural and diversity education as well. New Jersey and Delaware
have extensive content standards for world languages that are drenched
in culture, communication, and cultural context. The standards in New
Jersey, for example, are based on five core principles: "All students
should be able to communicate in at least one language in addition to
English; Culture is an integral part of world language learning; An effective world language class is student-centered; World languages should
start in kindergarten and continue uninterrupted through grade 12; and

World languages connect with all other disciplines." A number of states address the arts and the importance of cultural and political expression in and through the arts.

Mathematics and the sciences are also key places for serious attention to an authentic approach to multiculturalism. It is common for standards and frameworks to address mathematics and the sciences as if they held little or no multicultural content. Usually, however, there are areas at the beginning of the documents, at least in their introductions, where you can find official support for diversity curricula. Alberta, Canada, for example, introduces the common curriculum framework for mathematics with a discussion of beliefs about students and mathematics learning:

> Students learn by attaching meaning to what they do; and they must be able to construct their own meaning of mathematics. This meaning is best developed when learners encounter mathematical experiences that proceed from the simple to the complex and from the concrete to the abstract. The use of manipulatives can address the diversity of learning styles and developmental stages of students and can enhance the formation of sound, transferable mathematical concepts. At all levels, students benefit from working with appropriate materials, tools, and contexts when constructing personal meaning about new mathematical ideas. The learning environment should value and respect each student's way of thinking, so that the learner feels comfortable in taking intellectual risks, asking questions, and posing conjectures. (Alberta Learning Web site)

Similarly, Louisiana's science content standards include a statement on science and equity:

> The reform emphasis on science literacy has no boundaries. It excludes no one regardless of gender, race, ethnicity, and socioeconomic status. Unfortunately, because this has not always been the case in science education, it is not reflected in the enrollment in high school science classes and in the adult workforce of scientists. . . . It is imperative that reform science education in Louisiana include hands-on, inquiry-based science teaching that will develop thinking skills in all students for a lifetime of use. Preconceived notions that science has a very narrow scope and that it is limited to a select few can be dispelled by developing critical thinking skills in all students and by developing the practice of using these thinking skills in every area of life involving cognitive processes. Development of these skills begins with kindergarten

science explorations. . . . However, this philosophy is not enough to address the equity issue. Science education must also include keeping
students in contact with culturally appropriate role models and career
information. Reform efforts must dispel preconceived notions about
who can be a scientist. (Louisiana Department of Education Web site)

Also, the Louisiana mathematics framework carefully explains
how the framework itself is a model of multicultural action: in addition
to representatives from underrepresented groups in the development
process, a Louisiana equity review team reviewed the documents with
respect to students with learning disabilities, students with special education needs, minorities, students who speak English as a second language, and women.

Frameworks in mathematics and the sciences typically include a
common core goal of problem solving. The statement of goals will include attention to more diverse and complex problem-solving situations
that arise from relevant, real-life circumstances. Students are expected to
design problems growing out of complex, real-life situations and to generate appropriate solutions and decision options. Following the recommendations of the national associations in these areas, states and school
districts require that students experience a mathematics and science
curriculum in which topics are interconnected rather than taught in isolation; problems and procedures are connected to other subject areas
and to real-life, relevant situations that are challenging and motivating to
the students. The educational environment should encourage risk-tak-
ing, questioning, discovery, and collaboration. Teachers are expected to
listen carefully and value students' ideas, and the classroom community
is expected to be an exemplary model of a diverse learning community
that brings its discoveries to the attention of the larger community. Public presentations of relevant problem-solving projects are expected. The
key thing to note for these curricular areas is that the legal expectations
according to the standards suggest active involvement with the community in complex problem-solving tasks. Traditional, old-fashioned teaching and learning strategies are encouraged in support of an overarching
emphasis on meaningful learning in the community. It is in this respect
that the current standards and frameworks support serious multicultural
and diversity education within mathematics and the sciences.

Within the standards documents there are some specific areas of
mathematics and science that are ripe for diversity education. In the
area of data collection and analysis, students are typically expected to
comprehend statistical information and to apply statistical techniques
to interpreting problematic situations. In British Columbia, students in

grade 4 are expected to poll classmates and to analyze games of and challenges involving chance. In most states and provinces, students in all grade levels are expected to know and understand interrelationships among science, technology, and human activity, and how they affect the world. For example, in Connecticut, students analyze the possibilities and limits of science and technology in order to make and defend decisions about social issues, and they are expected to understand that the way in which scientific knowledge is formulated is crucial to the validity of that knowledge. They study the history of science and learn about how the evolution of scientific thought has influenced culture and society, and how groups from many countries have contributed to the diverse history of science (Connecticut Department of Education Web site).

Using the Standards to Achieve Multicultural and Diversity Education

An inclusive school community can be supported by state or provincial frameworks as well. Again, the standards are rarely meant to limit policy or practice, and are generally meant to encourage multicultural and diversity goals. Just to take one example, Vermont's framework includes an appendix of questions about the framework. In addressing the inclusive concept of "all students," this document legally supports school practices that are consistent with the framework, which is intended to provide a structure for curriculum-building and assessment of student learning, and to raise expectations for every student. A very small percentage of Vermont students may not meet the standards set forth in this framework because of the extreme severity of their disabilities. An example might be a high school student with a severe disability who functions at a pre-school academic level. Accommodations for such students should be specifically addressed in their individualized educational programs, within the spirit and context of what these standards intend.

> By all students, we mean specifically . . .
> ➼ Students who have been denied access to educational opportunities, as well as those who have not;
> ➼ Students who are female, as well as those who are male;
> ➼ Students who are African-American, Hispanic, Asian, American Indian, or members of other minorities, as well as those who are part of the racial or ethnic majority;
> ➼ Students who are socioeconomically disadvantaged, as well as those who are more advantaged; and

➤ Students who have not been successful in school, as well as those who have been successful. (Vermont Department of Education Web site)

To invite and enable many more students to reach high standards of performance, we need to make changes in our schools. Those changes will be many and difficult. Making them effectively requires that communities set high standards and hold themselves accountable for first-rate educational results for all students—no exceptions; no excuses.

In some curricular areas, there is little attention to multicultural issues. For example, physical education tends to overlook goals of inclusion and seems to ignore the notion that differently abled students might be participating in the physical education experiences of the school. In such cases, we can only turn to a general statement such as the one quoted from the state of Vermont, to suggest that we are meeting the expectations, and indeed exceeding them, in the application of the general principles of the documents to specific curriculum strands. These general statements would be generalizable, as well, to the contexts of "other diversities" that are pretty much ignored. Other than race, gender, and class, we will find hardly a mention of diversity. So it is up to the educator to interpret the general principle in terms of sexual orientation and other diversities. Administrators and teachers do this all the time. To pretend that the documents do not require attention to such diversity is to work against the political spirit of the diversity goals the documents lay out. To be apolitical or neutral in this sense is to make a political statement against diversity. To interpret the documents consistently is to take an important legal position.

Frameworks and standards can be used as bases for advocating multicultural and diversity curricula. The point is to do what you believe in because it is good practice, and to justify it with the legal expectations that such practice be done. You can explain your practice in terms of what the legal expectations are. The frameworks sometimes suggest multicultural/diversity curricula when read with a multicultural/diversity lens, but it's not so clear that this is really intended (e.g., Colorado economics framework, California science). Here you would intentionally read an interpretation into the standards in order to explicate how they can be implemented in your current context. Some approaches seem to preclude multicultural education (such as thinking of Spanish as a "foreign language"). This requires clever responses; but it is never unreasonable to go beyond the standards, or to apply a general statement from the introductory or summarizing remarks in order to explain your application of the standards to include a diversity agenda.

Some standards documents epitomize one of the classic approaches, like hero worship or an additive curriculum. Again, this is only a minimum expectation. A simplistic multicultural standard can be the catalyst for reconceptualizing how some special events or add-on curricula fit into the larger context (e.g., Cesar Chávez day can be part of a year-long curricular focus on civil rights). In general, the documents avoid explicit attention to multiculturalism and diversity issues. This might be to avoid the appearance of being "politicized"; framers worry about criticisms that have been unleashed when a small amount of attention to social justice has been present in such documents. The initial draft of the standards from the National Council for the Social Studies met with enormous controversy for trying to introduce multiple perspectives into the study of history. Yet we should note that most state and provincial documents clearly support the general ideas of multiple perspectives, along with cultural, social, or economic influences on the interpretation of these perspectives. It may be that educators simply need to explain what exactly has been passed as law in their state or province in order to help parents and community members understand what is going on in the schools and why.

The apparently "neutral" stance of many of the documents might also be understood as attention to the "disciplines." Diversity issues would be presumed to permeate anything that would appear in a list of content standards. The broader social justice goals would be implicit; yet they would not necessarily be mentioned under the presumption that multicultural and diversity education standards belong in a section of the document that belongs to all content. Nevertheless, we can suggest that there is a carefully orchestrated avoidance of diversity language in order to win broad popular support. This is not to say that the states are avoiding supporting multiculturalism/diversity, but rather that they leave it up to local school districts how the standards are to be interpreted in terms of curriculum and instructional practices, so that we can indeed interpret them according to the issues of this volume.

HIGH-STAKES TESTING

In general, people working for multicultural and diversity education can use standards to argue for many effective practices and policies. The standards often claim to be addressing "equity" and are therefore helpful in explaining reform efforts to parents and community members. However, the role of high-stakes testing, and the extreme warping of the curriculum in order to prepare for the tests, have dangerous implications for a diverse community. So, while we can work *with* the standards and frameworks, and while we may be able to *use* the tests as an excuse to implement many worthwhile practices, we know in the long run that the "discourse of accountability" is harmful to a pluralist, democratic society. Outside of reading, writing, mathematics, and science, it is difficult to convince an accountability-oriented public that current curricular practices are clearly directed toward performance improvement. For communities that are bent on "closing the gap" in test scores between white and nonwhite students, it is a challenge to emphasize what initially appears to be "extra frills." Money is bound to be micromanaged by school boards and administrators so that it is directed at test score improvement.

Educators must be creative in responding to the ongoing rhetoric of accountability. Amassing research that shows how financial investment in community building and diversity curricula pays off in the long run by saving the costs of later remedial programs is one productive direction. Another is to take advantage of the ongoing fear of violence in the schools. Surely, one could argue, a safe and secure facility is required in order for learning to occur. In this way, many diversity education programs can be combined with character education, civics instruction programs, peer mediation, and other efforts that are more clearly connected with reducing school violence.

Another important path for educators is explicit political action against the uses of testing and accountability in public policy. Students, parents, teachers, administrators, and other community members are increasingly demonstrating against the overwhelming use of high-stakes tests. Some students, parents, teachers, administrators, and other community members have participated in or supported boycotts; others have staged "street theater" in public sites condemning the harmful effects of these tests. Teachers and administrators have chosen to relocate in order to work in a community less committed to the tests. Parents have gathered resources with teachers and administrators to create charter schools or private alternatives that refuse to condone the abusive application of the potentially helpful standards and frameworks.

An excellent resource for political work against standardized testing is Alfie Kohn's Web site "Rescuing Our Schools from 'Tougher Standards.'" Kohn argues that a plague has been sweeping through American schools, wiping out the most innovative instruction and beating down some of the best teachers and administrators. Ironically, that plague has been unleashed in the name of improving schools. Invoking such terms as "tougher standards," "accountability," and "raising the bar," people with little understanding of how children learn have imposed a heavy-handed, top-down, test-driven version of school reform that is lowering the quality of education in this country.

Kohn's Web site supports the political efforts by some educators and parents to challenge the rhetoric of "standards"; in the worst cases, schools have become "giant test-prep centers, effectively closing off intellectual inquiry and undermining enthusiasm for learning (and teaching)." The most exciting aspect of this political movement is the slow understanding of many students, parents, teachers, administrators, and other community members that educational policy can be changed if people work within our democratic system to change it. Kohn includes information on why people should oppose the "tougher standards," what people can do to oppose these standards, contacts such as state coordinators of these efforts, and references and resources.

The Coalition for Educational Justice (CEJ) is one such regional group that has been active in the state of California. Members have attended school board meetings to argue for antiracist educational policy, collected information on diversity efforts and resources, and supported each other's efforts to promote antibiased, pluralist school programs. Their statement on high-stakes testing and retention policies in the Los Angeles Unified School District presents a strong case that such practices are class-biased and racist. Other efforts of the CEJ include working to cap class size at twenty in schools located in low-income communities, based on positive results of such policies in Tennessee, Wisconsin, and other areas; expanding the district's Academic English Mastery Program; establishing bilingual programs for African American students in order for them to learn Spanish and other languages; using the district's leverage to support affirmative action at the university level; expanding access to classes in ethnic studies, women's studies, labor studies, and a host of electives, with the input of teachers, students, and parents in developing curricula; ending racial profiling and militarism in the schools; and ending racism in public and mental health services by attacking racialized special education tracking in favor of real support for students with special needs and by guaranteeing toxic-free school sites for students.

Surely one of the most powerful ways that educators can influence policy and practice is by framing their own work in terms of multicultural and diversity issues. When new hires are made, we should consider their strengths and weaknesses in the light of diversity goals as well. It is important not to hire someone as a token representative of a minority group, but as someone who brings with them the skills and interests to promote diversity education. Your school should be active in the training of new teachers, bringing them in to work on multicultural projects, and establishing an ongoing source of new hires who understand the complexities and politics of diversity education. It is important to work for the legal rights of all educators in order to establish an effective and inclusive democratic school community. In general, the wise adage of multiculturalism should hold at all times: instead of making multiculturalism a special focus at a special time, it should always be integrated into any and all action. Every policy, event, classroom practice, curricular decision, and strategic plan should always question itself with respect to diversity: Is this an example of multicultural education? What can be modified to enhance the potential for promoting a diverse community? How can this be enhanced in order to support multicultural efforts? Can it be that racial and ethnic prejudices of educators are getting in the way? Might our presumptions about what is common sense (what must be done in order for the school to look like a school) be perpetuating insidious practices that undermine diversity and multicultural goals?

UNIONS

Unions and professional associations have important political and legal roles in the promotion of multicultural and diversity education. Rather than working as isolated individuals in a single school, educators and community members can work with and through unions to demand attention to multicultural issues, to require diversity policies as part of negotiated contracts, and to invite members of the community to participate in important decisions about educational programs. Unions also routinely profile multicultural and diversity efforts and are often able to provide support through national, state, or regional efforts for local projects. In the fall of 2001, for example, the American Federation of Teachers threw its weight behind President Bush's "Lessons of Liberty" initiative, which helps students learn more about our nation's history and values and encourages students to participate in community organizations and public service projects. In February 1999, the National Education Association published an article on the benefits of a racially diverse student body for elementary and secondary education (National Education Association Web site). The NEA has an active Minority Community Outreach Strategy, and the AFT has an ongoing program that helps its members and the community to focus their political action. As an example of what is available from professional associations, the National Council for the Social Studies maintains a Web site for using current events as teachable moments; although this site is most often used by social studies teachers, it can be an excellent resource for all educators concerned with contemporary social issues.

CHALLENGES TO MULTICULTURALISM

Multicultural and diversity education is challenged today by an increasingly conservative climate coupled with the enduring legacy of white supremacy, writes Priscilla Pardini (2000). There is a serious lack of diversity in teaching staff and educational leadership in the United States, and a depletion of funding for multicultural programs. School policies promote and perpetuate institutional racism. The standards movement measured with high-stakes testing pushes schools to adopt ever-narrowing views of learning and knowledge. "The result, say teachers and others working in K–12 classrooms, is a general waning in enthusiasm for and commitment to multicultural programs" (6). Educational consultants have witnessed a rapid decline of interest in professional development programs that focus on antiracist and multicultural education, and often need to "retool" their offerings in order to fit regressive interests in "closing the gap" in test scores. Closing the gap refuels conservative antidemocratic efforts by portraying minority groups as being in "need" of special help, thus returning the discussion of democracy and education to the premulticultural movement discourses of the early part of the twentieth century.

One key problem with constructing multiculturalism on the model of reform efforts of previous decades is that educators can mislead themselves into believing that they have "taken care of that issue." In fact, most schools in the United States claim to be doing something called multicultural education. In reality what they might be doing is something deleterious to the students or the community. Superficial levels of multiculturalism can be more harmful than helpful, as has been noted in earlier chapters. The focus of much teacher education has been reduced to "teaching tolerance"; by turning diversity education into collections of "multicultural methods" for classroom management, assessment, and instruction, teacher education unfortunately perpetuates hidden assumptions that "intolerable" features of "others" can be accommodated, altered, or assimilated into the invisible, dominant culture of "whiteness." Well-intentioned but misguided educators want to give students and faculty a "voice." Yet to give something implies an entrenched power hierarchy in the first place. Macedo and Bartolomé write,

In order to move beyond a mere politics of tolerance, educators will have to undergo a paradigm shift that will involve a de-emphasis on teaching methods as an end in themselves so as to fully understand how subordinated students learn in contexts characterized by economic exploitation, power asymmetries, racism, sexism, classism, and ethnic xenophobia. By refocusing on learning instead of teaching, educators will be able to develop a lucid clarity regarding the interrelationship between learning and teaching in order to realize that there is no teaching without learning and that learning ultimately determines and shapes teaching. (Macedo and Bartolomé 2000, 119)

Another challenge to multiculturalism comes from the confusion that arises in a democracy regarding the inclusion of "extreme groups." The expectation of diversity education is the active promotion of marginal views and a proactive concern for attending to the needs of members of marginal groups. But the question always arises: How do we include the groups that deny the interests and concerns of others? This is clearly an important issue in the politics of multicultural education. The religious right makes claims on public education that sometimes dovetail with conservative politics, and sometimes endanger the rights of others (for example, those with different sexual orientations). Fascist and antigovernment militia groups are suspicious of the goals of public schools. It is to be expected that cultural conflicts will become legal concerns for many educators, as the politics of education plays out in the specific location we call "school." Indeed, this is the job of educators: to become part of the cultural, political, and legal negotiations that compose the experience of schooling in the United States. Rather than seeing the politics as a problem to be dealt with, educators must understand the politics as part of what is interesting about their professional life. "Dealing with" the politics must be abandoned in favor of "working with" the politics. As an educator, you take on the politics as a professional challenge, and expect that your role to is make sure that the conversations, conflicts, and working solutions to specific crises include all constituents and potential perspectives on the issues involved.

In the aftermath of the terrorist attacks in the fall of 2001, some renewed interest in multiculturalism has surfaced. Yet this attention to diversity has more in common with the international and intercultural education movements of a century ago than with the progressive ideas of multicultural and diversity education that have evolved since the 1980s. For example, a need to understand different world languages has been identified as an important skill of globalization. This attention to language reconstructs problematic ideas about "foreign" languages rather than languages spoken by members of the global community and, indeed, of one's local community. As a result of the concern about security and nationalist movements, we have witnessed a rebirth in old-fashioned notions of identity that hide the realities of globalization and the multiplicity of identities that are parts of identity as a "learning process." This approach not only maintains the hidden assumptions of "tolerance," but undermines a politics of education that might promote global conceptions of social justice.

Carl Grant says that most multicultural programs are still mired in narrow foci (cited in Pardini 2000). They look only at one specific concern—say, language problems, girls' performance in mathematics, or African American participation in advanced classes. I suggest this might be caused by school bureaucracies: in order to justify funding for a specific project, those involved in the project need to make their claims so narrow as to be able to represent the success of their programs in the limited context of testing and score implications. What are needed are school and community efforts to pull all of these separate projects into a holistic conception of diversity efforts. Curtis Lawrence (2000) has described multicultural education in Milwaukee as devolving into "pockets of multiculturalism." The school district established district-wide learning goals that included students projecting antiracist, antibiased attitudes and participating in a multicultural curriculum. Lawrence points to the changing political climate, shifts in district leadership and vision, budget cuts, a move toward decentralization, and an increased emphasis on standards and testing as potential explanations for little change after a decade of experimentation with multiculturalism. Teachers interviewed noted that more of the kind of teaching held up as successful would be happening if there were encouragement from the administration, and especially if there were time for teachers to meet with one another during the school day. The pressures of testing and little time for preparation and developing new curricula are powerful forces.

As affirmative action is characterized by recent court decisions and ballot initiatives as "preferences that exclude," diversity educators must find new directions through which to support the participation of all members of society. As bilingual education continues to "substitute" for the politics of multiculturalism in ways that mischaracterize it (in terms of a focus on closing performance gaps rather than valuing democratic participation or the language and cultural skills that diverse members of the community bring with them to school), it serves to distract school boards and policy makers from issues of cultural democracy. As identity becomes increasingly questionable as a category for understanding diversity, multicultural education must re-assert itself more in terms of the *processes of relating* that are part of a multicultural and pluralist society and less in terms of specific outcomes that are to be achieved by a certain date. Politically, it must become acceptable for the goals of an initiative to be phrased in terms of these processes of inclusion and participation. The reality must be that diversity education is not a temporary focus. Diversity will never be a problem that can be solved simply so that we can move on to another immediate concern. Diversity is, rather, a source of possibilities and exciting changes that force us to always be recognizing our own self-imposed limitations that must be challenged. Multicultural education will always be here, always be "needed," and always be a central principle of vital educational programs.

REFERENCES AND FURTHER READING

Alberta Learning Web site. Mathematics. http://www.learning.gov.ab.ca/k_12/curriculum/bySubject/elem.pdf.

American Federation of Teachers Web site. http://www.aft.org/action/index.html.

California State Board of Education Web site. http://www.cde.ca.gov/board/pdf/history.pdf.

Coalition for Educational Justice. 2000. "High Stakes Testing and Retention Are Class-Biased and Racist." Available at http://www.fairtest.org/arn/High_Stakes_and_Retention_Are_Class_Biased_and_Racist.html.

Colorado Department of Education, Model Content Standards Web site. http://www.cde.state.co.us/download/pdf/civics.pdf.

Connecticut Department of Education Web site. http://www.state.ct.us/sde/dtl/curriculum/Cclsci.pdf.

Department of Veterans Affairs. 2001. "Lessons of Liberty Initiative." http://www.va.gov/Veteranedu/page.cfm?pg=5.

Donald, James. 1992. *Sentimental Education: Schooling, Popular Culture, and the Regulation of Liberty.* London: Verso.

Gitlin, Todd. 1995. *The Twilight of Common Dreams: Why America Is Wracked by Culture Wars.* New York: Metropolitan Books.

Kohn, Alfie. "Rescuing Our Schools from 'Tougher Standards.'" http://www.alfiekohn.org/standards/standards.htm.

Lawrence, Curtis. 2000. "Milwaukee: A Case Study." *Rethinking Schools: An Urban Educational Journal* 15, no. 1: 5, 8–9.

Louisiana Department of Education, Science Section II: The Teaching and Learning of Science—Science and Equity, http:/www.doe.statela.us/doe/publication/contents/stealear.htm.

Louisiana Department of Education Web site. http://www.doe.state.la.us/DOE/asps/home.asp.

Macedo, Donaldo, and Lilia Bartolomé. 2000. *Dancing with Bigotry: Beyond the Politics of Tolerance.* New York: St. Martin's Press.

"Multiculturalism: What Now? A Special Rethinking Schools Report." 2000. *Rethinking Schools: An Urban Educational Journal* 15, no. 1.

National Council for the Social Studies Web site. http://www.socialstudies.org/resources/moments/.

National Education Association. 1999. "The Benefits of a Racially Diverse Student Body in Elementary/Secondary Education." http://www.nea.org/publiced/racially.html.

National Education Association. Minority Community Outreach Strategy Web site: http://www.nea.org/partners/minority.html.

New Jersey Department of Education Web site. http://www.state.nj.us/njded/cccs/.

Ontario Ministry of Education/Ministry of Training, Colleges and Universities Web site. http://www.edu.gov.on.ca/eng/document/curricul/social/social.html.

Pardini, Priscilla. 2000. "Down but Not Out." *Rethinking Schools: An Urban Educational Journal* 15, no. 1: 4, 6–7.

Scott, Joan Wallach. 1989. "Multiculturalism and the Politics of Identity. In Micheline R. Malson, Jean F. O'Barr, Sara Westphal-Uhl, and Mary Wyers, eds., *Feminist Theory in Practice and Process.* Chicago: University of Chicago Press.

Torres, Carlos Alberto. 1999. *Democracy, Education, and Multiculturalism: Dilemmas of Citizenship in a Global World.* Lanham, MD: Rowman and Littlefield.

Vermont Department of Education. Framework of Standards and Learning Opportunities Web site. http://www.state.vt.us/educ/stand/framework.htm.

West, Cornel. 1993. "The New Cultural Politics of Difference." In Cameron McCarthy and Warren Crichlow, eds., *Race, Identity, and Representation in Education.* New York: Routledge.

Chapter Six

⚫⟶ Barriers to Multiculturalism

This chapter examines five types of assumptions about school practices that make it difficult for people to implement diversity education: assumptions about the grouping of students, economic and social reproduction, assumptions about the recruitment and training of teachers, assumptions about the culture of schools, and assumptions about school governance. These clusters of assumptions lead to traditional practices that create sets of relationships among curriculum, practitioners, students, family, and community members. In turn, these sets of relationships establish criteria for judging the legitimacy of institutional structures, commonsense expectations about what teaching and learning are supposed to "look like," and particular roles for certain members of the school community in decision-making and policy-setting processes. The final section of the chapter looks at the ideology of "tolerance" as the most serious barrier to educational change. If diversity education is to become an attribute of a school community, then it must take seriously the notion of dismantling traditions in inclusive and democratic ways. The community should establish ongoing investigations into how the vestiges of these traditions are creeping back into practices without notice; all committees and initiatives must examine their goals and processes with these potentially "harmful" traditions and antimulticultural expectations in mind. The school community must work to identify the implicit categories of knowledge about the institution that are readily available and legitimated in working groups and everyday practices. Indeed, the ways that we cut up the world clearly affect the way we organize our everyday life, writes Eviatar Zerubavel (1993):

> The way we divide our surroundings, for example, determines what we notice and what we ignore . . . the way we classify people determines whom we trust and whom we fear. . . . The way we partition time and space likewise determines when we work and when we rest, where we live and where we never set foot. (1)

GROUPING STUDENTS

Assessment and evaluation strategies enable us to categorize, compare, rank, and assign value to students' abilities and achievements in relation to one another and to students in other schools, states, and countries. Policymakers and educators in the United States and internationally have made categorizing students a central feature of schooling. It is important to realize, though, that the categories we use are not "real" in any "natural" sense. They are cultural expressions of our shared histories and at most represent the current state of power relationships and social structures of inequality. Deborah Goodman (2001) writes, "If school curricula already reflected our pluralistic society, we would not need 'multicultural' education. Instead schools and curricula reflect a society with a history of discrimination and oppression based upon race, sex, class, culture, religion, and sexual orientation" (3).

Educational groupings and categories are ideas and abstractions about human beings, their behaviors, and their attributes. For many years, the construct of "intelligence" went unquestioned by educators and social scientists, and was used to group and categorize students. More recently this construct has been challenged and adapted (into, for example, "multiple intelligences"). But along with intelligence, educators sort students by such hypothetical labels as achievement, creativity, motivation, ability, leadership, aspirations, and self-concept; unofficial but equally recognized in the research literature are constructs such as race, gender, sexual orientation, physical attractiveness, social class, English as a first or other language, and compliance with school rules.

Jeannie Oakes and Martin Lipton (1999) write, "it is tempting to accept the categories, explanations, and values that one's culture has constructed as real, true, and 'common sense,' but clearly they are not. As anthropologists remind us, each culture's meanings and values are simply the particular way a particular group of people has constructed solutions to questions and problems that arise as they create and preserve their society" (279–280). They note how many people compare Japanese and American definitions and valuing of "achievement" and "talent." Americans, it is said, pay greater attention to a student's "ability" and "talent" than their effort and persistence. A "good" student is typically synonymous with "smart student." In Asian cultures, it is more common for a "good" student to be "hardworking." As Oakes and Lipton note, there is no "true" answer to the question of what makes students good, even though many cultures treat the categories they construct and the meanings they assign to them as "common sense."

In the United States, most schools have decided that they can most sensibly respond to differences among students by separating them for instruction. Most schools use "homogeneous grouping" (students are in classes with students deemed to be most like each other). This includes age, academic ability, educational disadvantage, individual choice, prerequisite experiences, learning and behavioral disabilities, language proficiency, educational aspirations, and college potential. It is important for us to recognize, however, the strong overlap that these labels have with students' race, ethnicity, and social class. White and affluent students are disproportionately taught in classes for the high-ability and college bound. Defenders of homogeneous grouping base their hopes on teacher expertise in focusing techniques designed for specific types of students, and provide safeguards that their group assignment policies and practices are "color-blind" and "objective." They point to the accomplishment of the special programs that they run. But special classes—special education, gifted education, compensatory education, bilingual education—do as much to create differences as they do to meet the students' special needs. Many educators find instead that heterogeneous groups support multidimensional conceptions of intelligence, sociocultural theories of learning, constructivist approaches to teaching, and a community model of schooling. All of these conceptions fit well with diversity education goals. Problems occur when people expect schools to adopt such practices without looking different from those that are run on the special programs model. How schools make decisions about such grouping practices has strong implications for the diversity policy of the school community.

Common forms of sorting that occur in schools include tracking by ability, identifying gifted students, sorting by family background, sorting by postsecondary prospects, sorting by English language competence, sorting by disabilities, sorting by cognitive disabilities, and sorting by behavioral and emotional disabilities. Ability grouping or tracking is the routine organization of students into smaller homogeneous groups of high, average, and low students. Creative euphemisms that are designed to mask the negative placement in a lower category include "advanced," "accelerated," "opportunity," "basic," "SHARP," and "VISTA" programs. This form of sorting typically begins in the elementary years and continues through the grades. Grouping might occur for the entire day, or for specific subjects such as reading or mathematics. Commonly, it may consist of small ability groups following a staggered schedule so that each group gets time to be alone with the teacher.

Nearly all middle and high schools group students by ability, many for all academic subjects, based typically on student test scores and teacher recommendations, despite the strong research against the practice. Most schools would deny labeling a student as overall "low ability" or "high ability." Yet studies show an overwhelming overlap in the students who are in high-ability classes for one subject with high-ability classes in other subjects. Because earlier grades determine how far students can progress by the time they can graduate, students in the top classes in high school are likely to have been in such classes throughout their school years, and students who are not placed in high-ability groups early on have remote chances of ever moving into other groups. Students not placed in the uppermost of classes by the sixth grade will probably never complete calculus in high school. According to Patrick Shannon (1989), teachers in high-ability reading groups seldom interrupt students when working with them; 70 percent of reading is done silently, and students in these groups are often asked to read texts that are easy for them. Teachers of low-ability groups interrupted students between two and five times more often; 70 percent of reading is oral, and students are typically asked to read texts that are difficult for them to read. Differences in dress, deportment, manners, language, and language uses are mistakenly interpreted as intellectual deficits.

At some times in history, it was common for children considered "precocious" to skip grades. If they stayed with students of their own age or level, they would have most likely just adapted in some way or become extremely bored. About twenty states in the United States now provide special funding for "gifted and talented students," and nearly all schools have highly visible programs where the highest achieving students are grouped together for enrichment or accelerated instruction. This might happen through special "pull-out" programs, or within classes in special clusters. Mara Sapon-Shevin (1994) has written a strong condemnation of gifted programs for the ways in which they disrupt the school community and generally render school initiatives ineffective while purporting to be serving a special population. Other critics of such special groupings question why the special enrichment is only offered to a select few. They note that the types of challenges such enrichment offers are particularly appropriate for students who are often labeled as lower in traditional measures of ability, or they question the allocation of funding to such programs when other options might be available.

Compensatory programs aim to make up for deficits in children's life experiences. Popular in the 1960s, these programs were designed to "compensate" students whose poverty, home life, or other life circumstances left them with "cultural deficits." One theory still popular is that intensive remedial help early in a school experience can help students to "catch up" with their more advantaged peers. Schools with low-income students often have federally funded Title I programs that group the lowest achieving students for such special instruction, especially in reading and mathematics. Typically, Title I programs run as pull-out programs so that the low-achieving students are removed from the classroom for the special instruction while other students receive "less basic" curricular activities.

Gloria Ladson-Billings traces the language of deprivation back to the 1960s, in which seemingly positive goals of improving student and teacher effectiveness worked to create a perception that African American students were deprived, deficient, and deviant. More recently, deprivation has been replaced by the superficially innocuous term "at-risk." Who is at risk if not the same students who in the past were found lacking in some ways? Experiences and abilities in a different home language or dialect are disregarded or viewed as a detriment rather than as a resource. Experiences with family responsibilities, solving complex social problems, personal maturity, surviving in a hostile environment, and so on, are ignored. Deficit theories have indeed been debunked by studies that document the wide range of genre and function in the literacy practices of families and communities. Classic examples of this type of research include Shirley Brice Heath's (1983) study of the literacy in a poor black community (in which babies are held on the laps of adults who sit reading the newspaper on their front porches calling comments about the news over to their neighbors), Luis Moll and Norma Gonzales's (1994) descriptions of the "funds of knowledge" in the Latino community (community resources about school, church, auto repair, cultural history, health and medicine, and other areas of expertise), and Denny Taylor and Catherine Dorsey-Gaines's (1988) reporting on the strengths of African American children growing up in an inner-city community with the support of family and neighbors. What these studies and others demonstrate is that communities that appear poor in literacy and other academic skills can be rich in parallel literacy traditions, which are often untapped by the school curriculum. If teachers do not spend time in the community of their school learning about the rich traditions and vibrant sources of knowledge within their community, they are not prepared to work with their students. On the other hand, educators who work with community members to create a multicultural school curriculum will be able to use these kinds of knowledge as resources upon which their students can build.

ECONOMIC AND SOCIAL REPRODUCTION

A more appropriate theory for the "failure" of nonmainstream children can be found in the argument that schools reproduce the economic and social relations of society and therefore tend to serve the interests of the dominant classes. In this context, a result such as "70 percent of students in urban schools are dropping out" is understood not as a "coincidence" but as an "outcome" of the educational system. In this sense, students are accomplishing what the system intends: they are succeeding at failing school.

Tracking and other forms of grouping can result in practices where children have different educational experiences within the same classrooms or schools. Anne Dyson (1997) includes reputations, expectations, grade levels, retention, report cards, and standardized tests as factors in differential treatment of students. She writes, "sociocultural and linguistic differences can be institutionally framed as correlates of academic deficiencies, from the very start of a child's life" (11). Over the years of schooling, students who are initially similar in intellectual background and skills become increasingly different in achievement when schools put them into separate, ability-grouped classes. Students placed in lower-level classes (disproportionately Latino and African American students) consistently achieve less than classmates with the same abilities that the schools have placed in higher-level classes. Students with both high and low test scores perform better when they are in higher-level classes. Research on "detracked" classes shows not only that students who would otherwise be placed in low classes achieve far more in these mixed classes; high-achieving students can learn more in detracked classes as well (Oakes 1996; MacIver, Plank, and Balfanz 1998). Quite simply, research consistently shows that lower-ability classes do not promote learning, even if teachers believe they are applying their expertise in the most efficient manner; and such research also demonstrates that "higher-ability" students do not suffer from mixed classes, but instead outperform their peers who are placed in traditional, "advanced" classes. So it is hard to make a claim other than social reproduction in explaining the persistent use of tracking and other forms of grouping.

Yet schools rarely take the political risk of removing tracking systems from their institutions. Efforts by administrators and teachers to introduce detracked programs are often met with resistance from families who fear that their "advanced" children will lose the opportunities of higher-ability classes. In diverse communities there is often a concern that the "best" students might be scared away into private alternatives. When such reforms are successfully implemented, the community usually finds that most students perform better in the long run than those attending comparable schools in the region. Fears that the curriculum would be "watered down" are demonstrated to have been unwarranted.

The commonsense belief in grouping is so entrenched in our culture that we surely cannot accept it as merely unfortunate. It must be recognized as serving an economic purpose in an unjust society. Oakes and Lipton note,

> Arguments about whether to "fix" or largely abandon homogeneous grouping raise deep questions about how democratic schools should grapple with the differences among students. In a post-modern age—one with increasing student diversity—it becomes exceptionally difficult to specify what is mainstream (or normal) and what is different. It is increasingly hard to decide who is *really* special, and who is out of sync with traditional school practices. (Oakes and Lipton 1999, 308)

Resistance to detracking is a hot political issue. The anxieties about what will be lost for previously high-status students are enough to counter the overwhelming research evidence that the questionable advantages of grouping would be heavily outweighed by the advantages of more democratic alternatives. One important point, however, is that attempts to implement heterogeneous, or mixed, grouping must be prepared to respond not only to the entrenched fears but also to the long-held beliefs that justify the seeming efficiency of highly specialized categories and hierarchies. The prevalent norms of our society support the notion that education provides rewards to the "best" students. These best students "deserve" access to income, power, or status. Merely implementing mixed groups will not succeed and, indeed, will feed into public perceptions that the idea is crazy, if the people involved in the new groupings do not really believe in the efficacy of detracking. If people still believe that those who learn easily and quickly on their own are more intelligent than other students, or if there is inadequate development and discussion of new, democratic norms (of cooperation, support, and community; of knowledge, language, and culture), then educational reform will only serve to justify the inequities of grouping practices.

Heterogeneous classrooms directly challenge unarticulated attitudes and beliefs about race and social class. Curriculum guides, textbooks, legal requirements, teacher training, and media reports act as "filters" that maintain and support ideological and procedural commitments to grouping. Such filters prevent alternative or competing versions of knowledge from reaching educators and students. Heterogeneous grouping requires rethinking most aspects of schooling and community support.

RECRUITMENT AND TRAINING

The majority of potential teachers have not experienced years of multi-cultural education. This is an understatement. At best, a potential teacher is ready to imagine the possibilities for what multicultural education might look like. Indeed, who would enter a profession with the explicit purpose of seeking to do something other than what they themselves can imagine the job to entail? A small number of potential teachers do actually want to become teachers because they themselves have had negative experiences, or because they have familiarity with social injustice, and wish to be part of a democratic social project. But the overwhelming majority of teachers enter teaching hoping to re-create something that they themselves enjoyed as students, which could be taken to mean that they hope to re-create a seriously unjust and non-multicultural enterprise.

This is not to say that teachers are "bad"! Of course the majority of teachers believe in the potential of most children, and wish to do what they understand as "best" for the community in which they work. But the majority of potential teachers have little interest in entering a politically embroiled, hotly contested site of cultural and economic conflict. Most people seeking to become teachers are white and female, and come from nonurban environments (Yasin 1999). Most want to return to work in a community that is similar to the one in which they themselves attended school. They do not particularly seek to work with poor children, or in rural and urban schools serving nonwhite or non-English–first-language communities. They usually select the grade or content they wish to teach, and they apply to those schools in which they would like to work, generally avoiding the schools where the need for teachers is the greatest. They seek to work close to their home, which tends to be very much like the community in which they themselves attended school.

Teacher education experiences rarely change future teachers' attitudes and beliefs about poor and language-minority children. In fact, student-teaching experiences tend to reinforce whatever stereotypes and unstated beliefs they brought with them to the experience. Those predisposed to recognize strengths in urban and rural children and families will perceive these strengths during their student-teaching internships, but the majority will not; many potential teachers leave teacher education programs with stereotypes and negative images enhanced despite courses in multicultural education and required field experiences in urban and diverse environments. Although it is possible for a teacher to participate in a school community fully and to actively seek to learn about the neighborhoods involved in the school, most potential teachers seek time away from their professional life at home. Finally, seasoned teachers who are asked to work with future teachers and to mentor new teachers rarely have the expertise or understanding of multiculturalism that would be necessary to help novices to apply their comprehension of diversity to educational encounters.

Several policy responses have been suggested. Martin Haberman (1991) believes that those learning to teach must be adults who have had previous experiences working in diverse environments, and who study with classroom teachers who have been successful working in diverse settings with school programs informed by social justice goals. He believes that preparation for teaching cannot start until after one has a clear vision of what multiculturalism means for all citizens and its specific implications for the work of a teacher. And he believes that young people are not developmentally "ready" to understand classrooms in the social and political context that is needed. Haberman and many others have created post-baccalaureate teacher certification programs to attract adult career-changers to the teaching profession and to provide specific preparation for work in areas experiencing teacher shortages.

Others have established programs to recruit a more diverse pool of potential teachers, so as to make sure that the future composition of the hiring pool of teachers looks more like the students they will be teaching. Proponents of minority recruitment believe that teachers who have grown up in a community that is similar to the one that they work in will be better prepared to understand and respond to the community. One problem with this approach is that this pool of potential teachers does not have any more experience with multicultural forms of education than any other potential teacher. So although it is important to increase the diversity of a school's staff, it cannot be assumed that increased diversity of staff is automatically correlated with increased comprehension of diversity education reforms. There is merit to the notion that an African American teacher can be a good role model for African American students, a Latina teacher for Latino students, a Laotian American teacher for Laotian students; but it is also the case that these teachers would be good role models for all students, including white students. So the "best" nonwhite teacher candidates may be hired by more affluent schools, ironically making minority recruitment programs a tool of social privilege and undermining the goal of diversity education for all students.

State requirements for certification and accreditation requirements for certification programs in colleges and universities pay lip service to diversity issues. But they do not make this a central focus. Instead, they tend to reinforce expectations that teachers should be prepared in their subject matter and in scientific approaches to pedagogy. Thus, a candidate for a teaching job will most likely only be prepared for teaching in a just, pluralist society if they themselves have had additional experiences that prepare them in ways that the certification program did not.

Some school districts have set up partnerships with area colleges and universities. Future teachers work in extensive field situations in the district as part of their certification program; and graduates of the program get preferential treatment in the job application process. The theory is that these teacher applicants will understand the students in the school district and will have been prepared to teach the students better than candidates who may not have had such extensive experience with children in the district. Other districts require recently certified teachers to work first as aides. After a year or two as an aide, a novice may be considered for a position as a classroom teacher. This, too, works to guarantee extensive understanding of the particular district before a teacher begins work as the classroom teacher. However, aide positions tend to be low-paid, part-time (thus without benefits), and low in status; they may also violate union regulations. The largest problem with such programs is that they do not resolve teacher shortages, especially in districts that most need teachers prepared to work with poor and language-minority children.

The "answer," then, seems to be professional development. Teachers, administrators, and other school staff must grow through their work over time to develop the awareness, skills, and knowledge necessary to implement a democratic, pluralist educational program. Seasoned teachers as well as novices must find that the school community facilitates their learning from each other and from the students, family members, and others involved in the life of the students and the school. Elsewhere in this volume there are suggestions for incorporating active participation of staff and community members in ongoing examination of multicultural issues and possibilities. But like detracking, serious attention to professional development and active promotion of diversity education across the spectrum of the school community makes fantastic demands on the organization and bureaucracy of an educational institution. Time within teachers' workdays must be allocated for meetings. Space must be made for teachers to work together and with others on diversity projects and programs. Teachers, students, family members, and others need to be involved together in discussions about what is going on in their school. Oakes and Lipton are also helpful in this context:

What students accomplish in school is shaped by the school's organizational arrangements and routines, attitudes, and beliefs, and the relationships among everyone in the building. In other words, students need a school culture that makes it inevitable that all students receive a socially just and excellent education. So do teachers. (Oakes & Lipton 1999, 326)

SCHOOL CULTURE

Redefining school culture demands a redefinition of "school as we know it." Most schools are organized in hierarchical channels of authority and with careful attention to minding one's business. Teachers and students are not encouraged to get involved in someone else's problem, and fear retaliation for doing so. Rather than focusing on progressive efforts toward a reformed school community, schools typically attend to isolated incidents that pose problems for the administration or staff. Staff is asked to address one small, manageable issue at a time. Teachers and administrators feel overwhelmed by the never-ending requests and demands that are made of them. Administrators spend much of their time working to avoid potential lawsuits. Meetings are forums for passing on information and new expectations rather than for working together on redesigning school programs or for discussing challenging dilemmas. Ideological inconsistencies in school functions are left unquestioned in the interest of "getting on with the program." Separate groups of professionals each have their own turf of professional purpose and are careful to avoid trespassing on the work of others.

Oakes and Lipton describe five aspects of a school culture that consistently appear on lists of qualities shared by good schools. These conditions, which have an enormous impact on whether teachers will be able to teach well and students will be able to learn well, foster both high academic quality and social justice.

First, they mention that a school culture must "press everyone toward learning and social justice." Both learning and social justice must be at the core of the mission of the school and the ways in which everyone acts, so that even those who may not be considered "successful" in this context will have been affected or touched by the goals, and could express the importance of these goals. Instead of just saying that all students can learn, the school culture must be actively pursuing learning by all students. Instead of declaring the importance of others, the school culture must communicate implicitly that everyone is "the other," and "they" are "we."

Second, the school culture must provide broad and deep access to learning: the school must constantly assess how the curriculum can be richer, how every single student could be part of the most interesting and important parts of the curriculum, and how to advocate for more money to pay for the least-supported aspects of the school program.

Third, the school culture must build an environment of caring relationships. Caring communities are places where teachers can act on their deep commitments to knowing and caring for students. Smaller schools-within-schools and excuses to set up small personalized working groups, teams, and committees in and out of the standards curriculum are important parts of a successful school program. These smaller groups and committees would be formed with diversity in mind, and every effort would be made to check that they do not devolve into a new form of segregation. A schedule flexible enough to accommodate such efforts is essential to a positive school culture. Classes that stay together for longer periods of time, looping (teachers staying with children through several grades), and other efforts to build richer relationships require rethinking the school organization but pay off in the long run in terms of a caring community.

Fourth, teacher inquiry and activism must be supported by the school culture. This may take the form of action research that requires that the teacher be allowed to do something that has not been done before. It may mean classroom structures that enable teachers to spend more time just listening to what their students have to say. It may mean that time or money must be reallocated to support a special project. Instead of hiring "experts," it may serve the community more fully to establish dialogue groups or research teams that inform themselves and work alongside colleagues in reorganized classrooms. It definitely means encouragement of a critical attitude, and a welcoming of challenges to the status quo. Ongoing questioning of assumptions and periodic critique of even seemingly effective traditions and routines should be gratefully acknowledged.

Finally, the school culture must connect respectfully with communities. Typical "parent involvement" sets up parents as ancillary to the "real" work of schools or as deficient and in need of training in order to be better parents. Bridging the cultures of neighborhood and schools can work both to enhance the role of the school and to enhance the functions of "informal educational agents," such as alienated peers, discouraged families, and community resources. Traditionally, it has been the job of the family and community to demand a role in the school or to represent a nonmainstream interest. More recently, schools have welcomed a parent or community member who has an interest. But the most effective approach is for individual members of the school community to take it upon themselves to actively identify community resources, to personally educate themselves about community and diversity issues and events, and to make it clear through this work that they value the participation and contributions of all members of the community.

SCHOOL GOVERNANCE

A serious barrier to diversity education is the governance of schools. Systems of authority that employ top-down structures of administration at every level in the name of efficiency and productivity work against school cultures that foster democratic participation. It is clear that many areas of the United States separate clusters of schools from others in order to maintain the privileges experienced by those in the "better" schools. Why would a family move to a suburban community with "fine schools" if that community's schools were no different from the urban or rural schools nearby? Why would a taxpayer be interested in transforming schools so that every school in a district or state could be described as attaining the standards? Wouldn't this person question the expense of the community that supports the fancy school that they or their children attend? Schools are the tool of persistent segregation, sorting, and inequality. Because so much of the funding of schools is tied to revenue collection that is based on regressive property taxes, school districts must first look to local funding as a source of sustenance. Supplementary state or federal funding sources are also available; but local property taxes remain the primary source of school funding. Because property taxes are based on the value of homes and other taxable properties, suburbs enjoy a larger and more lucrative tax base relative to the size of their student populations. Rural regions with little industry, and urban centers occupied by millions of poor people in apartments and run-down housing, do not supply the same sort of tax base. In the last decade, some states have attempted to institute more equitable allocation of funds based on combinations of criteria. Yet these redistribution systems have had little effect on the overall funding for schools that serve poor communities or communities with diverse populations. Especially hurt are those communities that have made a commitment to diversity. Such communities have a wide range of socioeconomic demographics, so state formulas for school funding are skewed by the more affluent members of these communities—many of whom do not even attend the public schools. Average household income may have little to do with the realities of the tax base in a diverse community.

Tensions have arisen between professional control of schools through educationally trained administrators versus lay governance provided by a board of education with respect to student diversity; new models of school governance are considered for the effectiveness of teacher professionalism with respect to student diversity (Dunn 1998). Of particular concern is the role of family and community members in decisions about the schools. But there is no easy, perfect way in which to move toward democratic governance of schools. Community participation can mean that only connected, more privileged community members are involved, or that those with the means to be involved can determine the direction of school programs. Individual constituencies may have agendas that are inconsistent with multicultural and diversity goals.

One popular recommendation for educators is that they facilitate border crossings that promote successful collaboration among the various cultures of a school community. In "The Complex World of an Embedded Institution," Alan Peshkin (1995) delineates five categories of constituencies, all of which are formed by their type of interest in schools, the basis of that interest, and their relationships with seven subcategories of the beneficiary constituency. The impact, according to Peshkin, influences what schools do, what they should not do, what they should do better, and what they should do that is not currently done. As long as constituent interests and their extant pedagogical implications go uncontested, schools remain quiet; the status quo is taken as the proper order of things. If contested, interests become stakes, and stakeholders learn the boundaries of their interests, where they clash with those of others, and the extent of their own tendency to hold onto their own. According to this "clashing cultures model" of community involvement, no one culture can capture the "total picture" and each culture is, by the very fact of a constituency, partial. Peshkin (1995) writes, "Interests invest constituents in some dimension of schooling that usually is well short of the whole educational life of learners, educators, or schools. The partial nature of most constituent interests in schooling means, obviously, that most attend only to one aspect of school life. Attending to more than one aspect takes constituents beyond their interest, and, often, well beyond their expertise" (253).

If parents and families constitute a constituency, then, as Davies (1994) points out, minimal parent or family involvement in schools may be because this constituency has made little demand. Recent work in mathematics education indicates a significant lack of attention to collaborative family involvement by the profession (Peressini 1996, 1997); in the current "Principles and Standards" even less than before (National Council of Teachers of Mathematics 2000). Parents are typically positioned in standards documents as external supporters and little else. Yet, Davies notes the impetus for policy change in family involvement has come mainly from elites and policymakers, with minimal evidence of grassroots or consumer demands. Because families have not been involved in initiation, planning, or execution of new policies, Davies expects minimal benefits to disenfranchised "end-users."

A key component of family involvement is the active effort to avoid "managing" community members as potential sites of conflict and legal or political "trouble." Too often, educators fear the turmoil of politics. "Managing" parents and other community members by providing a minimal amount of "pretend involvement" in decision-making procedures can backfire by resulting in dissatisfaction and disaffection. In the "management model" this might be acceptable, as the alienated people are just as likely to give up on their efforts and either accept a more passive role in school governance or move to another school community. But a genuine effort toward multicultural and diversity education requires a kind of serious attraction to the conflicts that emerge, as they are indicative of important underlying sources of inequity and skewed dominance of the institution by combinations of constituencies. From the perspective of a critical multiculturalist, valuable resources and potential contributors to the community have been irrevocably lost by the management model. As Mary Henry (1996) notes,

> Listening to parents works, to a degree, for parents keep hoping that one day there will be some action and their voiced needs and demands will be met. The mere act of providing a space for parents to voice concerns works well in maintaining the status quo and achieving an equilibrium in the balance of power. The superintendent quietly reinforces a pattern of parental expression yet professional decision making [at board of education and open forum] meetings, where people are encouraged to voice concerns that will be considered by the board and the superintendent. (79)

Standardized testing, privatization, and charter school movements are relevant in this context. The establishment of standards and testing primarily serves a political aim to hide economic injustice rather than to promote higher quality or fairness. By declaring that each school will be held accountable for performance on a particular test of established standards, a government agency can masquerade as working toward equal educational outcomes for all students, when, in fact, the agency is continuing to label some schools (with particular characteristics) and some students (racially and economically tied to the characteristics of the underperforming schools) as inferior to others. Standards operate on the assumption that all students have an equal opportunity to learn. In reality, the playing field is anything but level. Enormous discrepancies exist among facilities, resources, and teachers in public schools—even within the same city or the same state—as a function of where one can afford to live. Curriculum standards alone will not ensure that everyone receives the same education. There is a strong concern among many researchers that standards will instead widen the gap between social classes in the United States. As long as affluent schools are reported as successfully meeting these standards when other schools do not, these affluent schools will be allowed to establish the meaning of the standards and the interpretation of what sorts of pedagogy are deemed appropriate for meeting the legal state or local goals.

One important criticism of the standards movement argues against standardization in general: standardization of outputs tends to lead to standardizing inputs; human variation is thus framed as a problem to contain. The rich variation in human differences becomes a problem in achieving standardization (Bohn and Sleeter 2000). Recent calls for federal attention to establishing "equal education" advocate what Dave Pushkin (2001) has described as "equivalent" education—"every child, regardless of contextualizing factors, mitigating circumstances, or confounding variables, would receive the same bare bones education and be assessed according to that curriculum. Schools and children are assessed as if every school starts from the same point and every child has the same foundation, even if it is not the case" (193). As Pushkin notes, the issue is not quantity of learning, but quality. For diversity educators, the quality of the experience is an outcome as well. Furthermore, to accept that school populations should remain segregated by race, class, and other categories of social difference is to declare support for social injustice and economic racism. On the one hand, as Pushkin writes, to demand "equivalent amounts" of education from all schools presumes that "poor" urban and rural schools are able to provide the same supplementary resources as suburban, affluent schools. When these schools cannot offer more than "the basics," advocates of federally mandated standards and testing define this as individual freedom; and they suggest we close down the schools that "fail" to achieve minimal scores on tests, in order to reopen them under the auspices of profit-making corporations. This point of Pushkin's is significant for diversity educators because they know that the "failure" of a school is really a success of a socially unjust system. The seeming "success" of the more affluent schools is more than just significantly higher scores on standardized tests: it is also the successful perpetuation of privilege for those students who "succeed." These seemingly "success-ful" students suffer from the lack of a multicultural education as well (by-products include fear of "others," little or no understanding of social justice, little or no experience in diverse social settings, a learned but in-accurate sense of superiority, and so on).

Recent efforts to support a diverse community by "closing the gap" in test scores only feed into the perpetuation of a system that is un-just and biased in the first place. It would be better to work against the reliance on test scores as the sole measure of success, even as schools seek to use these scores to acquire much-needed funding and other po-tential resources. A critical multiculturalist would work with members of the community to identify other forms of information to use in eval-uating school programs. Now, this recommendation could be misun-derstood as suggesting that some students cannot be expected to achieve the same standards as others, so that other criteria of "success" must be fabricated. But only a person who does not understand the fun-damental principles of multicultural and diversity education would come to such a conclusion: diversity education strives to surpass the ex-pectations of standards documents and tests of standardized curricula. As educators participate in decisions about school governance and the funding of education, they must keep this in mind. It is important to re-member that so-called minorities never get the chance to display their higher-order thinking skills and problem-solving talents. As victims of injustice they will often be called upon to display basic skills that for more affluent students are less important than research processes, crit-ical thinking, and problem posing. Parents will question the merits of new, innovative curricula if they do not appear to be providing the tra-ditional education they know their children will be called upon to demonstrate. Parents will suggest that the educators who chose the new curriculum expect that these children are not capable of mastering the "real" material. For these reasons, diversity educators must advocate full democratic participation in decisions, and must accept the viewpoints of community members as equal in importance to those of the "ex-perts." Educators should expect some well-intentioned and carefully re-searched innovations to be voted down in meetings and policy-making processes, in the long-term interests of cultural democracy.

Meanwhile, privatization of schools serves to further promote the mischaracterization of certain schools as desperately in need of special attention because of their population or location. Privatization also but-tresses the narrowing criteria of evaluating schools, reducing success to attainment of minimal scores on particular kinds of tests. According to Farrell (1994), "although urban public school educators are not achieving optimal results, there is no evidence that for-profit educational companies will do any better or possess special expertise in educating poor students of color. Education Alternatives, Inc., for example, has trouble retaining low-paid nonunion paraprofessionals and has cut out minority contractors; the Edison Project has no explicit multicultural curriculum" (72–75).

Charter schools, which have both democratic and antidemocratic aspects, mostly serve in this context to further undermine the efforts of educators in the public schools to create a genuinely pluralistic community. Charter schools need not serve this function. The creation and establishment of a charter school could have significant community-building components; and the school itself could be a model of multicultural goals. But in the larger context of the politics of educational governance, charter school policies tend to work in inconsistent ways that do not emphasize diversity aspirations.

THE IDEOLOGY OF TOLERANCE

By far the most serious barrier to educational change is the "ideology of tolerance" that is so pervasive in educational discourse. "Tolerance" is a common way in which multiculturalism is understood by the majority of people working with and in schools. It is fairly widely accepted that the United States has an increasingly diverse population, and that people must learn to accept each other as different if not to respect the actual differences. As was discussed in Chapter 5, multicultural and diversity education is challenged today by an increasingly conservative climate coupled with the enduring legacy of white supremacy. Within this climate, schools strive to "accommodate" diverse populations of students. The language of accommodation alone serves to denote the unequal distribution of power in school communities. Well-meaning educators, however, make valiant efforts to promote understanding and acceptance of differences. This ideology of tolerance, in which people believe that mere understanding of difference can lead to fair and equitable participation in democratic institutions, unfortunately hides deeply entrenched legacies of racial dominance, social class conflict, and the simplistic notions of identity carefully discussed in Chapter 5.

In the interests of tolerance and the avoidance of conflict, many educators avoid "highly politicized" words, or work to circumvent controversial issues. In the dominant Protestant Anglo culture, such social skills are the mark of a highly cultured and talented leader. But holding such values in leadership in high regard is itself a form of cultural, racial, and class power maintenance. Donaldo Macedo and Lilia Bartolomé (1999) call this kind of action in the name of tolerance "dancing with bigotry." They claim that tolerance for racial and ethnic groups as proposed by some white liberals not only constitutes a veil behind which they hide their racism, it also puts them in a compromising racial position. This is difficult criticism for people to take. Educators working for multicultural education declare in their daily actions that they are committed to an equal, democratic society with absolutely no discrimination on the basis of race, ethnicity, religion, sexual orientation, or disability. Yet these very actions may be received as a form of racism itself! This is because tolerance is a paternalistic idea. Tolerance implicitly means that nothing will really change. The hope is instead that everyone can now fit into the system and adapt to its expectations. The ideology of tolerance is a way of understanding how the world works that goes unquestioned by the majority of us as we live our lives, because it is the model by which we make meaning. We do not think about it because it is the way the world "is." But, in fact, it is not the way the world "is" for the majority of people in the world. Liberals are moved to "overcome" racial and other differences *that they can tolerate,* "by diluting them, by bleaching them out through assimilation or integration . . . the paradox is perpetuated: the commitment to tolerance turns only on modernity's natural inclination to intolerance; acceptance of otherness presupposes as it at once necessitates delegitimization of the other" (Goldberg 1996, 6).

The ideology of tolerance is evident in, for example, the minimal attempts to include "multicultural content" in the curriculum. It is made even more apparent in the ways that educators recoil in fear when these attempts are attacked as "unpatriotic" or "anti-American." What could be more patriotic than to represent the multiple and conflicting perspectives on the history of one's own country? What would be more American than to discuss the legacies of the Mexican-American war, for example, in defining Chicanos, when the story of the Southwest United States could so easily be told in terms of the "settlers" as "warriors" who seized land and set up institutions of domination that would last for generations? What would be more patriotic than to question the politics of bilingual education, and to lament the lost possibilities for a multilingual population if all students were encouraged to attend multilingual schools? In Canada, the Canadian Race Relations Foundation states quite bluntly that "Canada was established as an outpost of the British and French colonial empires. European culture projects by their nature always assumed cultural superiority on the part of the European colonizers, and the British and French efforts were no exception" (CRRF

E-Race It Web site). What would it mean for educational programs to be based on this statement?

The ideology of tolerance is evident as well in the ways that educators are forced to define their efforts to reform schools in terms of "new, improved methods" that will succeed with "all" students. A multicultural and diverse community is not necessarily achieved through "methods" of instruction. Indeed, a teacher's "methods" may have little to do with the impact that a school has on any given child. This may seem to contradict earlier chapters of this volume, in which different approaches to multicultural education are explained. The critical point here, however, is that diversity educators do not seek methods of instruction that have been proven successful in some scientific way. More fundamentally, toleration of difference must give way to embracing pluralist community participation, inefficient but effective governance, and multifaceted and complicated attempts to assess the instruments of assessment themselves. Multicultural and diversity education requires that we interrogate the ideology that is behind our methods. It challenges the notion that there is a best way to teach or to learn, and expects that a school community cannot just "buy into" a curriculum that "worked" somewhere else. What did they mean when they said it "worked"? Were their criteria informed by a serious commitment to a school as a cultural democracy?

QUESTIONS

The style of this book, even as a reference book, has shifted into a series of questions, because it is necessarily the case that any guide can only lead to new questions. The book itself was structured by initial questions I anticipated from the reader: What is multicultural and diversity education? What is the history of multicultural education? What are curricular examples of multicultural and diversity education? Can I see some case studies of multicultural and diversity education? Are there legal and political considerations? What are the most important barriers to achieving multicultural and diversity education? The following are questions, rather than answers, which serve to summarize the topics of this book:

Why do we believe that someone who learns faster learns better? Where does this belief come from, and why do we usually also believe that such behavior is a sign of something internal to the individual rather than an indication of privilege?

Why do you think it is so hard for people to value in their children the ability to work with and talk with everyone in their community? I would have thought that such skills would be essential. But it seems that those with privilege would prefer that their children be segregated in schools that train children of privilege to accept their fortune as the "way things work," and to value the perpetuation of privilege over even their own self-interests.

When someone claims to be working for diversity, he or she is often working merely for tolerance, because tolerance serves the status quo. It does not change the way things work. Real multicultural and diversity education means that we see evidence of serious changes in the way things work. Why is it impossible to achieve this? Why do people cling so strongly to knowing how things work? Why does this seem more comfortable than believing that your own community listens to you and cares about your participation in that community?

How can we work to create schools that support cultural democracy when those in political and economic power couldn't care less about the state of our schools? I know that industrial leaders are often seen to be committed to educational reform, but if they were so committed, would there not have been more changes by now? Clearly, despite the media rhetoric, education is less important than, say, the profits made in the oil industry, or the potential global market for computer chips. But this does not mean that schools cannot become a site of social change, which brings us back to the question at the beginning of this paragraph.

When are you going to have your first meeting that includes every potentially interested person in the school community?

Who will organize this meeting, and how will the choice of this person send a message to each participant in the community about who is in charge, who cares about them, and what is really possible as an outcome of this meeting?

Where will the meeting occur, and what will the choice of this location "say" to each participant in the community about who is in charge, who cares about them, and what is really possible as an outcome of this meeting?

What are two serious issues that you are afraid to discuss at this meeting, and why?

What are two fears you have about what will happen if such a meeting occurs, and why?

Why are you not taking the time to answer these questions?

What did you do after reading this book?

What did I leave out of this book?

How would my book be read as offensive by a certain person, and how could I reconsider the book in order to include the work of this person?

Can you think of a better way to organize this book that would be more consistent with its content and ethics?

Send your response to Appelbaum@arcadia.edu.

REFERENCES AND FURTHER READING

Bohn, Anita Perna, and Christine E. Sleeter. 2000. "Multicultural Education and the Standards Movement: A Report from the Field." *Phi Delta Kappan* 82, no. 2: 156–159.

Brice Heath, Shirley. 1983. *Ways with Words: Language, Life, and Work in Communities and Classrooms.* New York: Cambridge University Press.

Canadian Race Relations Foundation. E-Race It Web site. http://www.crr.ca/eraceit/default.htm.

Davies, Don. 1994. "Collaboration and Family Empowerment as Strategies to Achieve Comprehensive Services." In Leo C. Rigsby, Maynard C. Reynolds, and Margaret C. Wang, eds., *School-Community Connections: Exploring Issues for Research and Practice.* San Francisco: Jossey-Bass, pp. 267–280.

Dunn, Randy. 1998. "Professional Control and Lay Governance in Schools: Implications for Addressing Student Diversity." *Urban Review* 30, no. 1: 97–117.

Dyson, Anne Haas. 1997. *What Difference Does Difference Make? Teacher Reflections on Diversity, Literacy, and the Urban Primary School.* Urbana, IL: National Council of Teachers of English.

Farrell, Walter. 1994. "Will Privatizing Schools Really Help Inner-City Students of Color?" *Educational Leadership* 52, no. 1: 72–75.

Goldberg, David. 1996. *Racist Culture.* Oxford: Blackwell.

Goodman, Deborah. 2001. "Living (and Teaching) in an Unjust World." In Wendy Goodman, ed., *Living and Teaching in an Unjust World: New Perspectives on Multicultural Education.* Portsmouth, NH: Heinemann, pp. 1–25.

Haberman, Martin. 1991. "The Rationale for Training Adults as Teachers." In Christine Sleeter, ed., *Empowerment through Multicultural Education.* Albany, NY: State University of New York Press, pp. 275–286.

Henry, Mary. 1996. *Parent-School Collaboration: Feminist Organizational Structures and School Leadership.* Albany, NY: State University of New York Press.

Macedo, Donaldo, and Lilia Bartolomé. 1999. *Dancing with Bigotry: Beyond the Politics of Tolerance.* New York: Palgrave.

MacIver, Douglas, Steven Plank, and Robert Balfanz. 1998. *Working Together to Become Proficient Readers: Early Impact of the Talent Development Middle School's Student Team Literature Program—Report of the Center for*

Research on the Education of Students Placed at Risk. Baltimore, MD: Johns Hopkins University Press.

Moll, Luis, and Norma Gonzales. 1994. "Lessons from Research with Language-Minority Children." *Journal of Reading Behavior* 26, no. 4: 239–256.

National Council of Teachers of Mathematics. 2000. "Principles and Standards." Web site: http://www.nctm.org/standards/overview.htm.

Oakes, Jeannie. 1996. "Two Cities: Tracking and Within-School Segregation." In Ellen Condiffe Lageman and La Mar Miller, ed., Brown v. Board of Education: *The Challenge for Today's Schools.* New York: Teachers College Press.

Oakes, Jeannie, and Martin Lipton. 1999. *Teaching to Change the World.* New York: McGraw-Hill.

Peressini, Dominic. 1996. "Parents, Power, and the Reform of Mathematics Education: An Exploratory Analysis of Three Urban High Schools." *Urban Education* 31, no. 1: 3–28.

———. 1997. "Parental Involvement in the Reform of Mathematics Education." *Mathematics Teacher* 90, no. 6: 421–427.

Peshkin, Alan. 1995. "The Complex World of an Embedded Institution: Schools and Their Constituent Publics." In Leo C. Rigsby, Maynard C. Reynolds, and Margaret C. Wang, eds., *School-Community Connections: Exploring Issues for Research and Practice.* San Francisco: Jossey-Bass, pp. 229–258.

Pushkin, Dave. 2001. *Teacher Training: A Reference Handbook.* Santa Barbara, CA: ABC-CLIO.

Sapon-Shevin, Mara. 1994. *Playing Favorites: Gifted Education and the Disruption of Community.* Albany, NY: State University of New York Press.

Shannon, Patrick. 1989. *Broken Promises: Reading Instruction in Twentieth-Century America.* New York: Bergin and Garvey.

Taylor, Denny, and Catherine Dorsey-Gaines. 1988. *Growing Up Literate: Learning from Inner-City Families.* Portsmouth, NH: Heinemann.

Yasin, Said. 1999. *The Supply and Demand of Elementary and Secondary School Teachers in the United States.* Washington, D.C.: ERIC Clearinghouse.

Zerubavel, Eviatar. 1993. *The Fine Line: Making Distinctions in Everyday Life.* Chicago: University of Chicago Press.

Chapter Seven

◆ Associations and Organizations

The Algebra Project, Inc.
99 Bishop Allen Drive
Cambridge, MA 02139
Phone: (617) 491-0200
Fax: (617) 491-0499
http://www.algebra.org/index.html

A national literacy project founded by civil rights activist and mathematics educator Robert Moses. Aimed at low-income students and students of color, it emphasizes mathematical skills as a prerequisite for full citizenship.

American Indian Science and Engineering Society
P.O. Box 9828
Albuquerque, NM 87119-9828
Phone: (505) 765-1052
Fax: (505) 765-5608
http://www.aises.org

Provides teacher programs, curriculum programs, student programs, guidelines for American Indian/Alaska Native mathematics, science, and technology programs. Includes membership, professional chapter information, job listings, and an on-line newsletter that links to other Native American and multicultural websites.

Anti-Defamation League of B'nai B'rith (ADL)
823 United Nations Plaza
New York, NY 10017
Phone: (212) 490-2525
Fax: (212) 885-5855
http://www.adl.org

Organization dedicated to fighting anti-Semitism, bigotry, and extremism. Extensive resources and educational programs. The Web site includes links to related organizations and a search engine to aid in topic research.

Applied Research Center
3781 Broadway
Oakland, CA 94611
Phone: (510) 653-3415
Fax: (510) 653-3427
http://www.arc.org

Public policy, educational, and research institute that emphasizes issues of race and social change. Newsroom with recent press information, viewpoints, contemporary database, articles, and an archive.

Association of University Centers on Disabilities (AUCD)
8630 Fenton Street, Suite 410
Silver Spring, MD 20910
Phone: (301) 588-8252
Fax: (301) 588-2842
http://www.aucd.org

A network of interdisciplinary centers advancing policy and practice for and with individuals with developmental and other disabilities, their families, and their communities. Information on leadership education in neurodevelopmental and related disabilities; links to university centers for excellence and research centers for developmental disabilities; AUCD projects, resources, and employment opportunities.

Black Community Crusade for Children
25 E Street, NW
Washington, DC 20001
Phone: (202) 628-8787
Fax: (202) 662-3580
http://www.childrensdefense.org/bccc.htm

A program of the Children's Defense Fund that taps into the black community tradition of self-help. Promotes opportunities for children, community-building, spirituality, character and leadership development, intergenerational mentoring, interracial and interethnic communication, interdisciplinary networking, and training.

BUENO Center for Multicultural Education
University of Colorado
School of Education, Box 247
Boulder, CO 80309-0249
Phone: (303) 492-5416
http://www.colorado.edu/education/bueno

This program promotes quality education with an emphasis on cultural pluralism; facilitates equal educational opportunities for cultural and language-minority students; and disseminates research findings and related information through publications.

Campaign to End Homophobia
P.O. Box 382401
Cambridge, MA 02238-2401
http://endhomophobia.org

Nonprofit corporation with diverse, international support. Members include parents of lesbian and gay children, rabbis, priests, therapists, writers, community organizers, family planning staff, sexuality educators, AIDS activists, anti-oppression educators and diversity trainers, college students and their advisers, and lesbian, gay, and bisexual activists. Multicultural group focusing on learning about the relationships between homophobia/heterosexism and other forms of oppression and developing personal, cultural, and institutional strategies to educate themselves and others.

Canada Race Relations Foundation
4576 Yonge Street, Suite 701
Toronto, ON, M2N 6N4
Phone: (888) 240-4936 (toll free)
Fax: (888) 399-0333 (toll free)
http://www.crr.ca/rt/

A national agency that promotes a framework for fighting racism in Canadian society. The Web site contains publications, fact sheets, call-for-action proposals, bibliographies, a media center, and the "E-Race It" Web site for children, viewable in both French and English.

Canadian Ethnic Studies Association
43 Queen's Park Crescent East
Toronto, ON, M5S 2C3
Phone: (416) 979-2973
Fax: (416) 979-7947

http://www.ss.ucalgary.ca/ces/

Provides information about the association's journal, community news, students' corner, and biennial conference. The Web site is viewable in both French and English.

Catalyst Centre
720 Bathurst Street, Suite 500
Toronto, ON M5S 2R4
Phone: (416) 516-9546
(888) 521-1453 (toll free)
Fax: (416) 588-5725
http://www.catalystcentre.ca

A Canadian organization devoted to innovative learning, popular education, and research and community development that advances positive social change. Educational programs, resources, and an evolving "Popular Education Map"—a "database" of Canadian and international groups practicing popular education. Includes a calendar, news, resources, a bookstore, and consulting for public dialogue. Web site is viewable in both French and English.

Center for Multicultural Cooperation
P.O. Box 1385
Coarsegold, CA 93614
Phone: (800) 432-3618
http://www.activecitizenship.org

Provides civics curricula and professional development programs that focus on empowering America's youth. Includes information on the organization's curricula, materials related to civic values and service learning, and teacher training.

Center for Multilingual Multicultural Research
University of Southern California
Rossier School of Education
Waite Phillips Hall, Suite 402
Los Angeles, CA 90089-0031
Phone: (213) 740-2360
Fax: (213) 740-7101
http://www-rcf.usc.edu/~cmmr

Provides a base for those interested in multilingual education, English as a second language (ESL), language instruction, multicultural education, and related areas. Offers the opportunity to come together for research and program collaboration. Includes employment opportunities and links to related sites.

Center on Disability and Community Inclusion
University of Vermont
University Center for Excellence in Developmental Disabilities
    Education, Research, and Service (UCD)
101 Cherry Street, Suite 450
Burlington, VT 05401-4439
Phone: (802) 656-4031 (Voice/TDD)
Fax: (802) 656-1357
http://www.uvm.edu/~uapvt

This organization promotes the independence, inclusion, participation, and personal choice of individuals with disabilities of all ages in all environments. Develops culturally sensitive and responsive services and supports, interdisciplinary training, technical assistance, exemplary service models, research, dissemination of information, and advocacy for the legal and civil rights of individuals with disabilities.

Clearinghouse for Multicultural/Bilingual Education
Weber State University
Education Building, 3rd Floor
Ogden, Utah 84408
Phone: (801) 626-6000
http://catsis.weber.edu/MBE/HTMLs/MBE.html

Provides pre-kindergarten through postsecondary educators with commercial and noncommercial sources for multicultural and bilingual/ESL information, materials, and resources. Access to companies and organizations is included in their database.

Colorlines Magazine
4096 Piedmont Avenue, PMB 319
Oakland, CA 94611-5221
Phone: (510) 653-3415
Fax: (510) 653-3427
http://www.arc.org/C_Lines/ArcColorLines.html

Publication of the Applied Research Center that focuses on race, culture, and action.

Committee for Children
568 First Avenue South, Suite 600
Seattle, WA 98104-2804
Phone: (800) 634-4449
Fax: (206) 438-6765
http://www.cfchildren.org

Nonprofit organization dedicated to promoting the safety, well-being, and social development of children. Violence prevention, bullying, child abuse, and social-emotional literacy curricula. Programs for family and parent education. Includes information on grants and funding, statistics, and implementation support as well as employment opportunities.

Consortium on Inclusive School Practices (CISP)
Office of Special Education Programs, M. E. Switzer Building
330 C Street, SW
Washington, DC 20202
Phone: (202) 205-8888
Fax: (202) 205-8971
http://www.asri.edu/CFSP/brochure/abtcons.htm

CISP is a collaborative effort to build the capacity of state and local education agencies to serve children and youth with and without disabilities in school and community settings. The focus is on systemic reform rather than changes in special education systems only. Web site includes "issue briefs," monographs, links to change projects, and a connection to the Action Research Network.

Educational Justice
Justice Matters Institute
1375 Sutter Street, Suite 110
San Francisco, CA 94109
Phone: (415) 353-5735
Fax: (415) 353-5733
http://www.edjustice.org

Promotes access to quality education for students from all racial and cultural groups. "Conversations" forum, resources, curriculum materials. The Web site features student work in an on-line gallery and includes a calendar of meetings and events, conferences, and performances.

Enabling Education Network (EENET)
University of Manchester, Educational Support and Inclusion

Oxford Road, Manchester M13 9PL
Phone: 44 (0)161 275 3711
Fax: 44 (0)161 275 3548
http://www.eenet.org.uk

EENET is an information-sharing network aimed at supporting and promoting the inclusion of marginalized groups in education worldwide. The Web site includes newsletters and links by topic to on-line documents, bibliographies, and other resources on policy, deafness, child-to-child activities, inclusion, teacher education, action learning, and early childhood.

Facing History and Ourselves
16 Hurd Road
Brookline, MA 02445
Phone: (617) 232-1595
Fax: (617) 232-281
http://www.facing.org/facing/fhao2.nsf

Provides interdisciplinary programs, resource materials, and speakers for middle and high school educators to relate the past to issues in the world today, civics education, and history as a moral enterprise. The Web site includes a calendar of events.

Gay, Lesbian, and Straight Education Network (GLSEN)
121 West 27th Street, Suite 804
New York, NY 10001-6207
Phone: (212) 727-0135
Fax: (212) 727-0254
http://www.glsen.org/templates/index.html

National network of parents, students, educators, and others fighting to end discrimination based on sexual orientation and gender identity/expression in kindergarten through high school. The Web site includes extensive resources, news, updates, announcements of events at the action center, and links to related efforts.

Highlander Research and Education Center
1959 Highlander Way
New Market, TN 37820
Phone: (865) 933-3443
http://www.hrec.org

Organization devoted to overcoming poverty, bigotry, and economic injustice in Appalachia and the South by working on "root causes." General information, initiatives, resources, news.

Illinois Association for Multilingual Multicultural Education
1855 Mt. Prospect Road
Des Plaines, IL 60018-1805
Phone: (847) 803-3112
http://www.iamme.org

Professional association promoting high-quality educational policies and practices for potentially English-proficient learners; supports multilingualism and multiculturalism. The Web site includes related links and employment opportunities.

Institute for Global Ethics
11 Main Street
P.O. Box 563
Camden, ME 04843
Phone: (207) 236-6658
Fax: (207) 236-4014
http://www.globalethics.org

Promotes ethical behavior in individuals, institutions, and nations through research, public discourse, and practical action. Decision skills curriculum materials available.

Inventors Assistance League
403 S. Central Avenue
Glendale, CA 91204
Phone: (818) 246-6546
Fax: (818) 244-1882
http://www.invention.org/culture/index.html

Celebrates the resourcefulness of inventors of all cultures and both genders in advancing technology and making our world what it is today.

Iris Films
2600 Tenth Street, Suite 413
Berkeley, CA 94710
Phone: (510) 845-5414
Fax: (510) 841-3336
http://www.irisfilms.org

Nonprofit documentary film company dedicated to U.S. and international social issues; materials designed to challenge people to examine their own beliefs and work toward change.

Media Awareness Network
1500 Merivale Road, Third Floor
Ottawa, ON, K2E 6Z5
Phone: (613) 224-7721
(800) 896-3342 (toll free)
Fax: (613) 224-1958
http://www.media-awareness.ca/eng/issues/minrep/resource/
teachunt.htm

Provides teaching units and student handouts having to do with the portrayal of diversity. These resources are downloadable from the Web site.

Multicultural History Society of Ontario
43 Queen's Park Crescent East
Toronto, ON, M5S 2C3
Phone: (416) 979-2973
Fax: (416) 979-7947
http://citd.utsc.utoronto.ca/mhso/index.htm

Works with communities, schools, cultural agencies, and institutions to preserve, record, and make accessible archival and other materials that demonstrate the role of immigration and ethnicity in shaping the culture and economic growth of Ontario and Canada. Web site includes current projects and conference information.

The Multicultural Skyscraper
On-Line/More Colour in the Media Foundation
P.O. Box 1234
3500 BE Utrecht
The Netherlands
Phone: 31 30 230 2240
Fax: 31 30 230 2975
http://www.multicultural.net

Provides information on media and minorities worldwide in a creative format.

Multiculturalism in Canada
Mount Allison University
Centre for Canadian Studies
15 Eddy Street, Seventh floor
Hull, Quebec, K1A 0M5

Phone: (819) 994-1315
Fax: (819) 994-1314
http://www.pch.gc.ca/csp-pec/english/about/multi/index.htm

Provides history and discussion of ethnic and racial diversity, multicultural policy, and prospects for the future. Web site is viewable in both French and English.

National Association for the Advancement of Colored People (NAACP)
4805 Mt. Hope Drive
Baltimore, MD 21215
Phone: (877) 622-2798
http://www.naacp.org

Nation's largest and strongest civil rights organization. Resources, action center, news. Web site includes details on ongoing programs and a search engine.

National Association for Multicultural Education
733 15th Street, NW, Suite 430
Washington, DC 20005
Phone: (202) 628-6263
Fax: (202) 628-6264
http://www.nameorg.org

Advocates for educational equity and social justice. Active organization in the field. Web site includes conferences, publications, state chapters, resources, links.

National Coalition for Parent Involvement in Education (NCPIE)
3929 Old Lee Highway, Suite 91-A
Fairfax, VA 22030-2401
http://www.ncpie.org

NCPIE is a coalition of education, community, public service, and advocacy organizations working to create meaningful family-school partnerships. Information on developing partnerships, disabilities education, state parent centers, and resources for family involvement.

National Coalition of Education Activists
P.O. Box 679
Rhinebeck, NY 12572
Phone: (845) 876-4580

http://www.nceaonline.org

Multiracial network of families, school staff, union and community activists, and others organizing for equity and fundamental changes in local school districts. Supports activists in developing, promoting, and implementing progressive school reforms, counters the right, and fights racism and other forms of institutional bias.

National Association of State Boards of Education
277 S. Washington Street, Suite 100
Alexandria, VA 22314
Phone: (703) 684-4000
Fax: (703) 836-2313
http://www.nasbe.org/Educational_Issues/Diversity.html

The association's website holds reports and policy briefs on diversity issues, including assessment of students with limited English proficiency, bilingual education, cultural competence, desegregation in an era of standards-based reform, and the education of migrant students. Provides a report entitled "The American Tapestry: Infusing Multiculturalism into American Education" along with links to organizations and research information.

National Institute for Urban School Improvement
Center for Marketing, Networking, and Utilization
55 Chapel Street
Newton, MA 02458
Phone: (617) 969-7100, ext. 2105
Fax: (617) 969-3440
http://www.edc.org/urban

Promotes inclusive schools. Web site includes a "library," e-news, publications, an urban forum, and an events database. Occasional links to articles on themes of inclusion.

National Organization on Disability (NOD)
910 Sixteenth Street, NW, Suite 600
Washington, DC 20006
Phone: (202) 293-5960
Fax: (202) 293-7999
http://www.nod.org

NOD promotes the full and equal participation of America's 54 million men, women, and children with disabilities in all aspects of life. Includes extensive resources on community, employment, education, politics, transportation, religion, health care, and technology.

Northwest Educational Regional Laboratory Equity Center
Northwest Regional Educational Laboratory
101 S.W. Main Street, Suite 500
Portland, OR 97204
Phone: (503) 275-9603
http://www.nwrel.org/cnorse/index.html

Formerly the Center for National Origin, Race, and Sex Equity, this organization helps schools and communities with an equity information line and publications and resources on equity and technology, urban education, gender-specific programming for girls, and links to other equity sites.

Parents, Families, and Friends of Lesbian, Gay, Bisexual, and Other Transsexual Persons (PFLAG)
1726 M Street, NW, Suite 400
Washington, DC 20036
Phone: (202) 467-8180
Fax: (202) 467-8194
http://pflag.org

PFLAG "promotes the health and well-being of gay, lesbian, bisexual, and transgendered persons, their families, and their friends through: support to cope with an adverse society; education to enlighten an ill-informed public; and advocacy to end discrimination and secure equal civil rights. PFLAG provides an opportunity for dialogue about sexual orientation and gender identity, and acts to create a society that is healthy and respectful of human diversity."

Partnership for Family Involvement in Education (PFIE)
U.S. Department of Education
400 Maryland Avenue, SW
Washington, DC 20202-8173
http://pfie.ed.gov

Administered by the U.S Department of Education, PFIE offers resources, ideas, funding, and conferences through its programs "Employers for Learning," "Community Organizations," "Religious Groups," and "Family-School Partnerships." Its Web site includes information on membership in the partnership, building partnerships, current federal initiatives, publications, and partner activities.

Pedagogy and Theater of the Oppressed
P.O. Box 31623
Omaha, NE 68131-0623
http://www.unomaha.edu/~pto

Information on the annual conference devoted to critical thinking and social justice. Programs based on the work and goals of Augusto Boal and Paulo Freire.

Primary Source
125 Walnut Street
Watertown, MA 02472
Phone: (617) 923-9933
http://www.primarysource.org

Nonprofit center for the interdisciplinary study of history and the humanities. Professional development programming that aims to be historically accurate, culturally inclusive, and explicitly concerned with racism and other forms of discrimination.

Rethinking Schools
1001 E. Keefe Avenue
Milwaukee, WI 53212
Phone: (414) 964-9646
Fax: (414) 964-7220
http://www.rethinkingschools.org

Publishes an educational journal begun by Milwaukee teachers devoted to rethinking schools and communities. Resources and other links.

Southern Poverty Law Center
400 Washington Avenue
Montgomery, AL 36104
Phone: (334) 956-8200
http://www.splcenter.org

Combats hate, intolerance, and discrimination through education and litigation. Web site includes details of their KlanWatch and militia task force, and links to the *Teaching Tolerance* magazine.

Syracuse Cultural Workers
P.O. Box 6367
Syracuse, NY, 13217
Phone (315) 474-1132

Fax: (877) 265-5399
http://www.syrculturalworkers.org

Tools for change: feminist and progressive materials; peace, justice, and community-building products and resources.

Teachers First

Network for Instructional TV, Inc.
11490 Commerce Park Drive
Reston, VA 20191-1532
Phone: (703) 860-9200
Fax: (703) 860-9237
http://www.teachersfirst.com/multicult.htm

Resources from a variety of disciplines suitable for use in multicultural settings.

Teaching for Change

Network of Educators on the Americas (NECA)
P.O. Box 73038
Washington, DC 20056
Phone: (800) 763-9131 (toll free)
Fax: (202) 238-0109
http://teachingforchange.org

NECA is a Washington, DC–based nonprofit organization that promotes social and economic justice through public education. Multicultural resources; "Behind the Headlines" current issues curriculum ideas; ongoing professional development projects.

Theater of the Oppressed Laboratory

122 West 27th Street, Tenth Floor
New York, NY 10001
Phone: (212) 924-1858
Fax: (212) 674-6506
http://www.toplab.org

New York–based interactive theater workshops for social change. Includes a bibliography, a photo gallery, information on ongoing projects and upcoming events, internship opportunities, and related links.

Women's Equity Resource Center

55 Chapel Street
Newton, MA 02458-1060

Phone: (617) 969-7100
(800) 225-3088
Fax: (617) 332-4318
http://www.edc.org/WomensEquity

National project that promotes bias-free education, believing that gender equity works for everyone—for girls and women, men and boys. The mission is to increase educational opportunities and outcomes for all students by focusing on gender equity and drawing on the strength of gender, race, ethnicity, disability, and income.

Chapter Eight

⋗ Print and Nonprint Resources

This chapter includes annotated bibliographies on community building, curricula, multicultural and diversity education, "talking points" for
generating discussions and promoting action planning within meetings, and finally, nonprint resources devoted to social justice and diversity education.

COMMUNITY-BUILDING RESOURCES

Cartledge, Gwendolyn, and JoAnne Milburn, eds. 1994. *Teaching Social
Skills to Children: Innovative Approaches.* 3d ed. New York: Allyn and
Bacon.

Tools for developing social skills in children through adolescence,
across a broad range of backgrounds and abilities; practical applications, examples, strategies, and suggestions for intervention.

Developmental Studies Center. 1996. *At Home in Our Schools.* Oakland,
CA: Developmental Studies Center.

Schoolwide activities that help educators and parents create caring
school communities. Contains ideas about leadership, step-by-step
guidelines for fifteen activities, reproducible planning resources, and
suggestions for teachers.

———. 1996. *Ways We Want Our Class to Be: Class Meetings that Build
Commitment to Kindness and Learning.* Oakland, CA: Developmental
Studies Center.

Well-respected resource for teachers on effective strategies for classroom meetings.

Drew, Naomi, and Susan Remkus, eds. 1995. *Learning the Skills of*

Peacemaking: K–6 Activity Guide on Resolving Conflict, Communicating, and Cooperating. Rolling Hills Estates, CA: Jalmar Press.

Effective classroom strategies for facilitating students' communication skills and creating peace in the classroom.

Kriete, Roxanne. 1999. *The Morning Meeting Book.* Greenfield, MA: Northeast Foundation for Children.

A daily routine that brings students and teachers together in a circle to greet one another, to share and respond to each other's news, to think together, to play together, and to look forward to the events in the day ahead.

Sapon-Shevin, Mara. 1999. *Because We Can Change the World: A Practical Guide to Building Cooperative, Inclusive Classroom Communities.* Boston: Allyn and Bacon.

Practical strategies for inclusive classrooms and supportive environments for young children. Cooperative games, children's literature selections and activities, songs; responses to teasing, bullying, and exclusion; racism, poverty, students with disabilities.

Wood, Chip. 1999. *Time to Teach, Time to Learn: Changing the Pace of School.* Greenfield, MA: Northeast Foundation for Children.

Offers meaningful ways to transform the quality of teaching and learning for all children through a reconsideration of our use of time.

Woodfin, Libby. 1998. *Familiar Ground: Traditions that Build School Community.* Greenfield, MA: Northeast Foundation for Children.

Discusses how the Greenfield Center School, NEFC's K–8 laboratory school, uses traditions like all-school meetings, mixed-age games, and partner lunches to create a strong sense of whole-school community. Descriptions of the traditions are accompanied by guidelines for implementing these traditions in other settings.

CURRICULUM RESOURCES

Adams, Maurianne, Lee Bell, and Pat Griffin, eds. 1997. *Teaching for Diversity and Social Justice: A Sourcebook for Teachers and Trainers.* New York: Routledge.

Resources that address communication and understanding between members of diverse social groups. Provides a unified framework by which students can engage and critically analyze several forms of social oppression and discrimination.

Andrus, Lucy. 2001. **"The Culturally Competent Art Educator."** *Art Education* 54, no. 4: 14–19.

Art teachers have a responsibility to develop and implement culturally responsive curricula even though their training experiences may not have involved multicultural education.

Barton, Angela Calabrese, and Marjorie Osborne, eds. 2001. *Teaching Science in Diverse Settings: Marginalized Discourses and Classroom Practice.* New York: Peter Lang.

Essays on liberatory science education, the social construction of science and identity, and systems of race, class, and gender oppression and domination. Explores practice and curriculum for diverse learners; the role of marginalized discourses; the meaning of "science for all."

Bigelow, Bill, and Bob Peterson, eds. 1998. *Rethinking Columbus: The Next 500 Years.* 2d ed. Milwaukee, WI: Rethinking Schools.

A revised and expanded edition of a popular booklet that changes the way "the discovery of America" is taught in classroom and community settings.

Boal, Augusto. 1992. *Games for Actors and Non-Actors.* New York: Routledge.

A handbook of theater games, exercises, and methods from the creator of Theater of the Oppressed.

———. 2001. *Legislative Theatre: Using Performance to Make Politics.* New York: Routledge.

Using performance to ask people what they think about government in order to help them be part of social change.

Christensen, Linda. 2000. *Reading, Writing, and Rising Up: Teaching about Social Justice and the Power of the Written Word.* Milwaukee, WI: Rethinking Schools.

Language arts teaching for justice. Includes essays, lesson plans, and a collection of student writing; designed for staff development and teacher education.

Conway-Turner, Kate, et al., eds. 1998. *Women's Studies in Transition: The Pursuit of Interdisciplinarity.* Newark: University of Delaware Press.

Addresses the need for women's studies to cut across disciplines, to continually redefine and develop methodologies, and to focus on issues facing women and women's creative scholarship.

Derman-Sparks, Louise. 1989. *Anti-Bias Curriculum: Tools for Empowering Young Children.* Washington, DC: National Association for the Education of Young Children.

Practical suggestions for early childhood curriculum development.

Diaz Soto, Lourdes. 2001. *The Politics of Early Childhood Education.* New York: Peter Lang.

Challenges the sanctity of Western views of early childhood.

Dillard, Angela. 2001. *Guess Who's Coming to Dinner Now? Multicultural Conservatism in America.* New York: New York University Press.

Places diversity and multiculturalism in a broader perspective by recognizing the increasing diversity of conservative groups in the United States.

Finazzo, Denise Ann. 1997. *All for the Children: Multicultural Essentials of Literature.* New York: Wadsworth.

Innovative textbook that examines children's literature through diversity and genre.

Gibbs, Jeanne. 1999. **"Guiding Your School Community to Live a Culture of Caring and Learning: The Process Is Called Tribes."** Windsor, CA: Center Source Systems.

A pamphlet for administrators based on a popular text by the same author.

———. 2001. *Tribes: A New Way of Learning and Being Together.* 6th ed. Windsor, CA: Center Source Systems.

How to teach essential collaborative skills, design interactive learning experiences, work with multiple learning styles, foster the development of resiliency, and support school and community change.

Gregson, Bob. 1983. *The Incredible Indoor Games Book: One Hundred and Sixty Group Projects, Games, and Activities.* Fearon Teacher Aids. New York: McGraw-Hill Children's Books.

Sourcebook for inclusive physical education and problem solving.

———. 1984. *The Outrageous Outdoor Games Book: 133 Group Projects, Games, and Activities.* Fearon Teacher Aids. New York: McGraw-Hill Children's Books.

Sourcebook for inclusive physical education and problem solving.

Grineski, Steven. 1996. *Cooperative Learning in Physical Education.* Chicago: Human Kinetics.

Proven ideas that promote positive interdependence, individual accountability, and collaborative skills.

Hoose, Philip. 1993. *It's Our World, Too! Stories of Young People Who Are Making a Difference.* Boston: Little, Brown.

Accounts of children working for human rights, the needy, the environment, or world peace; and a handbook for young activists, with practical suggestions for planning, organizing, publicizing, and raising funds for social action projects.

Kuharets, Olga R., ed. 2001. *Venture into Cultures: A Resource Book of Multicultural Materials and Programs.* 2d ed. Chicago: American Library Association.

The contributors provide short essays and recommended children's books (with suggested grade levels included), Web sites, videos, audiotapes, and directions for programming that cover the cultures of people in Africa, the Caribbean, India, Korea, Latin America, the Middle East, and Russia as well as Americans of Indian and Jewish heritage.

Lee, Enid, Deborah Menkart, and Margo Okazawa-Rey. 1998. *Beyond Heroes and Holidays: A Practical Guide to K–12 Anti-Racist Multicultural Education and Staff Development.* Washington, DC: Network of Educators on the Americas.

Many practical suggestions for creating dialogue, lesson plans, and so on.

Lewis, Barbara, Pamela Espeland, and Caryn Pernu. 1998. *The Kid's Guide to Social Action: How to Solve the Social Problems You Choose—*

And Turn Creative Thinking into Positive Action. Minneapolis, MN: Free Spirit Publishing.

Illustrative stories of kids who care and do social justice, and guides to the skills involved, including sample forms (petitions, letters, news releases, etc.) and a resource guide with addresses and phone numbers.

Luvmour, Sambhava, and Josette Luvmour. 1990. *Everyone Wins! Cooperative Games and Activities.* New York: New Society Publishers.

Well-respected collection of "new games" and cooperative activities that build community and foster cooperation.

Milford, Susan. 1992. *Hands around the World: 365 Creative Ways to Build Cultural Awareness and Global Respect.* Charlotte, NC: Williamson.

More of an international perspective than a multicultural perspective, this popular collection of activities might be useful to a diverse, multicultural community.

Minkler, John. 2001. *Active Citizenship: Empowering America's Youth.* Coarsegold, CA: Center for Multicultural Cooperation.

Social studies and civics for seventh through twelfth grades. Political problems; civic values; dialogue and conflict resolution; current political problems. Active learning and critical thinking. Also, materials available from the same group for teacher training and service learning.

Richard-Amato, Patricia, and Marguerite Ann Snow. 1992. *The Multicultural Classroom: Readings for Content-Area Teachers.* New York: Longman.

Textbook designed for prospective secondary teachers, with both general chapters about secondary education, and curriculum-specific suggestions.

Schneidewind, Nancy, and Ellen Davidson. 1997. *Open Minds to Equality: A Sourcebook of Learning Activities to Affirm Diversity and Promote Equality.* 2d ed. Boston: Allyn and Bacon.

A well-respected resource that addresses the violence of discrimination on the basis of gender, class, age, sexual or religious preference, ethnicity, and physical abilities. Also includes an extensive resource section. Although recommended for upper elementary through high school students, the activities can be modified for younger children.

Sleeter, Christine, and Carl Grant. 1999. ***Turning on Learning: Five Approaches for Multicultural Teaching Plans for Race, Class, Gender, and Disability.*** 2d ed. Upper Saddle River, NJ: Merrill.

Textbook that presents "before" and "after" lesson plans to demonstrate how teachers can change their lessons to fall within five categories of approaches to multicultural education.

Strange, Johanna, and Merita Thompson. 1991. ***Discover: Skills for Life.*** Circle Pines, MN: American Guidance Service.

Levels K–6 available; integrates character education and conflict resolution into the general curriculum.

Thul, Robert. 1997. ***Math for a World that Rocks.*** Chicago: St. Ignatius College Prep.

Twenty-three math-justice investigations for eighth through twelfth grades.

Trentacosta, Janet, and Margaret Kenney, eds. 1997. ***Multicultural and Gender Equity in the Mathematics Classroom: The Gift of Diversity.*** Reston, VA: National Council of Teachers of Mathematics.

Issues and perspectives, classroom cultures, curriculum, instruction, and assessment; professional development, future directions, bibliographic references.

Zaslavsky, Claudia. 1997. ***The Multicultural Math Classroom: Bringing in the World.*** Portsmouth, NH: Heinemann.

Elementary and middle-school mathematics lessons based on mathematical techniques from around the world. More of an international perspective than a multicultural perspective.

GENERAL WORKS

Adams, Maurianne, Lee Anne Bell, and Pat Griffin, eds. 1997. ***Teaching for Diversity and Social Justice: A Sourcebook for Teachers and Trainers.*** New York: Routledge.

Uses an integrated approach to oppression and social justice to present theoretical foundations and frameworks, illustrative samples of classroom and workshop activities, and print and video resources; focuses on increasing communication and understanding among diverse and unequal social groups.

Alperson, Myra. 2000. *Dim Sum, Bagels, and Grits: A Sourcebook for Multicultural Families.* New York: Farrar, Straus, and Giroux.

A guide for parents of adoptive families, useful to educators. Balancing birth and adoptive culture; shaping a multicultural home; alternative to the family tree; facing and addressing anti-ethnic and anti-adoptive prejudices.

Banks, James, ed. 1996. *Multicultural Education, Transformative Knowledge, and Action: Historical and Contemporary Perspectives.* New York: Teachers College Press.

A textbook on multicultural education that takes a historical perspective on types of knowledge, roots of multiculturalism, and links to transformative teaching; surveys pioneering scholars in the field, with a focus on women scholars and activists of color.

Banks, James, and Cherry McGee Banks, eds. 2000. *Multicultural Education: Issues and Perspectives.* 4th ed. New York: John Wiley and Sons.

A textbook for present and future educators on becoming effective practitioners in culturally, racially, and language-diverse classrooms and schools. Includes a glossary and a list of resources.

———. 2001. *Handbook of Research on Multicultural Education.* New York: MacMillan.

Compilation of major theory and research from the last thirty years. Includes chapters on history, goals, research, and key issues in the field; immigration and ethnic groups in historical and social science research; language issues, academic performance, intergroup relations; higher education; and international perspectives on multicultural education. Cross-referenced by subject and name indexes.

Boal, Augusto. 2001. *Hamlet and the Baker's Son: My Life in Theatre and Politics.* New York: Routledge.

Memoir from the creator of the Forum Theatre, the Legislative Theatre, the Rainbow of Desire, and other explorations of audience activity. A good introduction to Boal's range of ideas for theater activism.

Books, Sue, ed. 1998. *Invisible Children in the Society and Its Schools.* Mahwah, NJ: Erlbaum.

Essays examine groups of children and young people largely unseen and unheard: homeless children and their families; white working-class girls subjected to domestic violence; children and young people orphaned and otherwise affected by AIDS; immigrant children; urban Appalachian children; adjudicated girls; teenage mothers; and gay and lesbian youth. By sharing the voices of the young, providing basic information about particular groups of children and young people, and offering thoughtful analysis of their social situation, the book works to combine advocacy with scholarship.

Brunner, Diane Dubose. 1998. *Between the Masks: Resisting the Politics of Essentialism.* Lanham, MD: Rowman and Littlefield.

Proposes a multicultural revision of knowledge that replaces binarisms of insider/outsider as opposed to shifting the margin to the center. Studies representation and the politics of place; resists essentialist politics through the identity marking/making role of cultural materials.

Bruno-Jofré, Rosa, and Natalia Aponiuk, eds. 2001. *Educating Citizens for a Pluralistic Society.* Calgary, Alberta: Canadian Ethnic Studies Association.

Collection of Canadian writers on four themes: historical and philosophical perspectives on the impact of globalization on citizenship education; group rights and schooling; multicultural and antiracist education; and decoding cultural images in the classroom.

Campbell, Duane, and Delores Delgado-Campbell. 1999. *Choosing Democracy: A Practical Guide to Multicultural Education.* 2d ed. New York: Prentice Hall.

A textbook for future and current teachers that takes a reconstructionist approach to advocating democratic school reform. Teaching alternatives that respond to issues of racism, sexism, gender, and class bias.

Chase, Clifford. 1998. *Queer 13: Lesbian and Gay Writers Recall Seventh Grade.* New York: Rob Weisbach Books.

Not only relief and anger but nostalgia, in a collection of ruminations on the junior high school experience.

Cohen, Linda. 1998. *Meeting the Needs of Gifted and Talented Minority Language Students.* Silver Spring, MD: National Clearinghouse for Bilingual Education.

Although labeling students gifted and talented can be understood as undermining the goals of diversity education, this helpful collection of suggestions is relevant if taken critically.

Cole, Robert. 1995. *Educating Everybody's Children: Diverse Teaching Strategies for Diverse Learners.* Lincoln, NE: Association for Supervision and Curriculum Development.

Report of the association's Urban Middle Grades Network, Advisory Panel on Improving Student Achievement, and Improving Student Achievement Research Panel.

Cortes, Carlos. 2000. *The Children Are Watching: How the Media Teach about Diversity.* New York: Teachers College Press.

Mediamakers as multicultural curriculum developers; mass media and multicultural learning; struggling with stereotypes; multicultural education in the cyberspace era.

Crawford, James. 1989. *Bilingual Education: History, Politics, Theory, and Practice.* Trenton, NJ: Crane Publishing.

A textbook for foundations courses in bilingual education; includes legal requirements for bilingual education, pertinent court cases that have impacted the education of LEP students, and a comprehensive history of bilingual education in the United States.

Delpit, Lisa. 1995. *Other People's Children: Cultural Conflict in the Classroom.* New York: New Press.

Sometimes dubbed "multicultural education with a human face," this analysis of what is happening in U.S. classrooms argues that many children of color are bearing the brunt of miscommunication as schools and "other people's children" struggle with the imbalance of power and the dynamics of inequality plaguing our social systems.

Gay, Geneva. 2000. *Culturally Responsive Teaching: Theory, Research, and Practice.* New York: Teachers College Press.

Students will perform better on multiple measures of achievement when teaching is filtered through their own cultural experiences and frames of reference. Includes teacher caring; teacher attitudes and expectations; formal and informal multicultural curriculum; culturally informed classroom discourse; and cultural congruity in teaching and learning strategies. Interweaves personal stories.

Goodman, Wendy. 2001. *Living and Teaching in an Unjust World: New Perspectives on Multicultural Education.* Portsmouth, NH: Heinemann.

Essays that seriously discuss empowerment of students in democratic classrooms in the "real world" (where family structure is fluid, varied, and changing; where students live in mansions, duplexes, projects, or cars; where parents work in factories, fast-food restaurants, farms, or universities; where educators value lifelong learning and value every member of the school community).

Hollinger, David. 2000. *Post-Ethnic America: Beyond Multiculturalism.* New York: Basic Books.

A historian, Hollinger argues that even as multiculturalism has brought a needed awareness and respect for ethnic and other diversity, the movement is overgrown, overgeneralized, and beset with increasingly apparent drawbacks and excesses. He calls for a more world-based citizenship, up-to-date with the contemporary appreciation for ethnocultural diversity, except that a postethnic United States would emphasize transitory, transnational, and voluntary forms of affiliation.

hooks, bell. 1994. *Teaching to Transgress.* New York: Routledge.

Classic black feminist perspective on teaching for freedom.

Kincheloe, Joe, and Shirley Steinberg. 1997. *Changing Multiculturalism: New Times, New Curriculum.* London: Open University Press.

Surveys critical multiculturalism, including educational purpose; power and democracy; hegemony, representation, and justice; class, gender, and race; and white studies.

Kivel, Paul. 1996. *Uprooting Racism: How White People Can Work for Racial Justice.* Gabriola Island, BC: New Society Publishers.

A guide for white people struggling to understand and end racism while supporting antiracism work. Moves beyond the definition and unlearning of racism to address privilege for white people; suggests ways for individuals and groups to challenge the structures of racism. Exercises, questions, and suggestions for social action.

Ladson-Billings, Gloria. 1994. *The Dreamkeepers: Successful Teachers of African American Children.* San Francisco: Jossey-Bass.

Examines eight exemplary teachers who differ in personal style and methods but share an approach to teaching that affirms cultural identity. Portraits that promote intellectually rigorous and culturally relevant classrooms for all children.

Lauter, Paul. 1991. *Canons and Contexts.* New York: Oxford University Press.

Critical examination of proposals to reform higher education. Concrete examples of a comparative method for teaching literary texts and integrating curricula.

Letts, William, and James Sears, eds. 1999. *Queering Elementary Education: Advancing the Dialogue about Sexualities and Schooling.* Lanham, MD: Rowman and Littlefield.

Collected essays that examine how children's lives are damaged by homophobia; suggests initial ways that educators can begin to transform educational practice.

Macedo, Donaldo, and Lilia Bartolomé. 2000. *Dancing with Bigotry: Beyond the Politics of Tolerance.* New York: St. Martin's Press.

Uses examples from mass media, popular culture, and politics to illustrate the larger situations facing U.S. educators in the midst of an "ethnic and cultural war." Argues that the popular press and mass media educate more people about issues regarding ethnicity and race than all other sources of education available to U.S. citizens; sheds light on the ideological mechanisms that shape and maintain the racist social order.

Mahalingam, Ram, and Cameron McCarthy, eds. 2000. *Multicultural Curriculum: New Directions for Social Theory, Practice, and Policy.* New York: Falmer Press.

Various authors build a new paradigm for teaching multiculturalism. Argues that current epistemological and pedagogical practices designed to forward multiculturalism actually serve antithetically by essentializing cultures. Offers alternative theories, classroom teaching methods, and policies.

Marable, Manning, ed. 2000. *Dispatches from the Ebony Tower: Intellectuals Confront the African American Experience.* New York: Columbia University Press.

Writers, poets, historians, and academics. Illustrates Marable's claim that the black intellectual tradition has always been descriptive, presenting the reality of black life and experience from the point of view of blacks themselves. Challenges and critiques racism and stereotypes.

McLaren, Peter, and Carlos Ovando. 1999. *The Politics of Multiculturalism and Bilingual Education: Students and Teachers Caught in the Cross-Fire.* New York: McGraw-Hill.

Textbook of collected writings that takes a critical perspective on the implications for education of a country increasingly divided along class lines: brown, urban, and multilingual with a teaching force composed mostly of white, middle-class females. Good introduction to a range of contemporary writers in the field. Related publisher-sponsored Web site.

McLaren, Peter, and Christine Sleeter, eds. 1995. *Multicultural Education, Critical Pedagogy, and the Politics of Difference.* Albany, NY: State University of New York Press.

Impressive collection of authors writing on multicultural education theory and practice.

Moses, Robert, and Charles Cobb. 2001. *Radical Equations: Math, Literacy, and Civil Rights.* Boston: Beacon Press.

Memoir by the founder of the Algebra Project; personal narrative and impassioned argument for new kinds of education reform as the legacy of the civil rights movement.

National Association for Multicultural Education. *Multicultural Perspectives.* Mahwah, NJ: Erlbaum.

Quarterly journal published by the association.

National Association of State Boards of Education. 1992. *Winners All: A Call for Inclusive Schools.* Report of the NASBE Study Group on Special Education. Alexandria, VA: National Association of State Boards of Education.

Guide to fundamental shifts in instruction, teacher preparation, and certification programs necessary for the realization of inclusive schools; uses examples and "checklists for action."

Nieto, Sonia. 1999. *The Light in Their Eyes: Creating Multicultural Learning Communities.* New York: Teachers College Press.

Applies research in learning styles, multiple intelligences, and cognitive theories to place "learning" at the center of multicultural education as a transformative process. Discusses social contexts, equity, culture, and critical pedagogy.

———. 2000. *Affirming Diversity: The Sociopolitical Context of Multi-cultural Education.* 3d ed. White Plains, NY: Longman.

Explores personal, social, political, cultural, and educational factors in the success or failure of students. Provides a conceptual framework and suggestions for implementation of multicultural education.

Oakes, Jeannie, and Martin Lipton. 1999. *Teaching to Change the World.* Boston: McGraw-Hill.

Textbook that provides a uniquely critical and engaged overview of the teaching profession. Infuses issues of diversity throughout.

Perry, Theresa, and Lisa Delpit. 1998. *The Real Ebonics Debate: Power, Language, and the Education of African-American Children.* Milwaukee, WI: Rethinking Schools.

Educators, linguists, and writers examine the political nature of language and its inseparability from race and class in the United States. Includes a history of Ebonics; essays by famous writers.

Schoem, David, ed. 1993. *Multicultural Teaching in the University.* Westport, CT: Praeger.

Edited volume with chapters on multiculturalism across campuses.

Secada, Walter, Elizabeth Fennema, and Lisa Byrd Adajian, eds. 1995. *New Directions for Equity in Mathematics Education.* New York: Cambridge University Press.

Examines research and practice in mathematics education from the standpoint of equity. Includes model programs; feminist theory; social and cultural perspectives.

Seller, Maxine, and Lois Weis, eds. 1997. *Beyond Black and White: New Faces and Voices in U.S. Schools.* Albany, NY: State University of New York Press.

Essays from people who are usually not heard from, probing "familiar minorities," "newcomer minorities," and "other minorities." Historically silenced voices introduce a new sense of diversity.

Shohat, Ella, ed. 2001. *Talking Visions: Multicultural Feminism in a Transnational Age.* Cambridge, MA: MIT Press.

Multivoiced essays from activists, scholars, artists, and curators chal-

lenging traditional disciplinary boundaries. Presents "relational feminism"; forges connections among knowledge, activism, alliances, and
epistemologies.

Sleeter, Christine. 1996. *Multicultural Education as Social Activism.* Albany, NY: State University of New York Press.

Argues that multicultural education is a political quest for social
justice rather than a technical issue of how to accomplish diversity. Examines what multicultural education means to white people;
self-reflexive analysis of race and gender in defining the meaning of
multiculturalism.

Sleeter, Christine, ed. 1994. *Empowerment through Multicultural Education.* Albany, NY: State University of New York Press.

Collection of essays that demonstrate that multicultural education can
both empower individuals and transform society.

Sleeter, Christine, Carl Grant, and Deborah Stollenwerk, eds. 1999. *Making Choices for Multicultural Education: Five Approaches to Race,
Class, and Gender.* 3d ed. Upper Saddle River, NJ: Merrill.

Historical and conceptual textbook that offers five different ways of understanding the implementation of multiculturalism.

Southern Poverty Law Center. *Teaching Tolerance Magazine.* Montgomery, AL: Southern Poverty Law Center.

Free to educators at http://www.teachingtolerance.org/.

Spring, Joel. 2000. *Deculturalization and the Struggle for Equality: A
Brief History of the Education of Dominated Cultures in the United
States.* 3d edition. New York: McGraw-Hill.

A very brief history of the education of Native Americans, Puerto Ricans,
Mexican Americans, African Americans, and Asian Americans. Multicultural perspective that places current debates in historical context. Examines deculturalization, integration, segregation.

Steinberg, Shirley, and Joe Kincheloe, eds. 2001. *Multi/Intercultural
Conversations: A Reader.* New York: Peter Lang.

International collection of essays on education and social justice; examines education as a global endeavor.

Stephan, Walter, and James Banks. 1999. *Reducing Prejudice and Stereotyping in Schools.* New York: Teachers College Press.

Explores theory and research; contact theory; and improving intergroup relations.

Syracuse Cultural Workers. *Peace Calendar.* Syracuse, NY: Syracuse Cultural Workers.

Annual calendar with monthly themes of peace and justice and related print and internet resources. Teaching guide by Mara Sapon-Shevin also available.

Tatum, Beverly. 1999. *Why Are All the Black Kids Sitting Together in the Cafeteria?* Rev. ed. New York: Basic Books.

Examines self-segregation as a problem and a coping mechanism. Explores why people are reluctant to talk about race.

Trinh T. Minha. 1989. *Woman, Native, Other: Writing, Postcoloniality, and Feminism.* Bloomington: Indiana University Press.

Examination of third-world feminist literature and literary theory.

Weil, Danny. 1998. *Towards a Critical Multicultural Literacy.* New York: Peter Lang.

Discussion of theory and practice that encourages the quest for self-examination through social transformation; students can confront the challenges of the diversity of everyday life through reasoning when educators create relevant problem-posing activities.

TALKING POINTS

Banks, James, Peter Cookson, Geneva Gay, Willis D. Hawley, Jacqueline Jordan Irvine, Sonia Nieto, Janet Ward Schofield, and Walter G. Stephan. 2001. **"Diversity within Unity: Essential Principles for Teaching and Learning in a Multicultural Society."** *Phi Delta Kappan* 83, no. 3: 196–203.

"What do we know about education and diversity, and how do we know it? This question guided the work of a Multicultural Education Consensus Panel, sponsored by the Center for Multicultural Education at the University of Washington and the Common Destiny Alliance at the University of Maryland. The article is the product of a four-year project during which the panel, with support from the Carnegie Corporation of New York, reviewed and synthesized research related to diversity. Two psychologists, a political scientist, a sociologist, and four specialists in multicultural education identified twelve essential principles. The principles are organized in the article into five categories: (1) teacher learning; (2) student learning; (3) intergroup relations; (4) school governance, organization, and equity; and (5) assessment." (http://depts.washington.edu/ centerme/dwu.htm)

Byres, Deborah, and Gary Kiger. 1996. *Common Bonds: Anti-Bias Teaching in a Diverse Society.* 2d ed. Wheaton, MD: Association for Childhood Education International.

This book is acclaimed by teachers as giving useful advice on how to be an unbiased teacher and responding to controversial situations in schools.

Christian, Karen M. 2001. **"The Issues of Diversity and Multiculturalism in Preschool Education: A Reader's Theatre."** *Multicultural Education* 9, no. 1: 30–32.

This brief script is suitable for reading at the beginning of a discussion and raises a collection of important issues related to multiculturalism, family, and community involvement.

Feliciano, Cynthia. 2001. **"The Benefits of Biculturalism: Exposure to Immigrant Culture and Dropping Out of School among Asian and Latino Youths."** *Social Science Quarterly* 82, no. 4: 865–879.

This article reports on an examination of how retaining an immigrant culture affects school dropout rates among Vietnamese, Koreans, Chinese, Filipinos, Japanese, Mexicans, Puerto Ricans, and Cubans. Those who enjoy the greatest educational success are not those who have abandoned their ethnic cultures and are most acculturated.

Jesness, Jerry. 2001. **"Not Just for Foreigners Anymore."** *Education Week* 21, no. 13: 32, 34.

Jesness sets up multiculturalism as mostly "bogus," and argues that those who are bi-, tri-, or multilingual hold the key to understanding other cultures.

Maalouf, Amin. 2001. *In the Name of Identity: Violence and the Need to Belong.* Translated by Barbara Bray. New York: Arcade Publishing.

Written before the terrorist events of September 2001, but acclaimed as prescient by a number of reviews, this book argues that a politics of identity based on a sense of victimization—which reduces identity to a single affiliation—facilitates the creation of "identities that kill." Discussing how people create "otherness," the author writes from a position of multiple identities about multiple identities.

Morris, Marla. 2001. **"Multiculturalism as Jagged Walking."** *Multicultural Education* 8, no. 4: 2–8.

Teaching multiculturalism presents problems, as many students exhibit fierce resistance—especially around issues of racism. Morris proposes a new model that examines the multidimensionalities of place and memory as they shape multicultural identities.

"Multiculturalism: A Fight for Justice." 2000. *Rethinking Schools* 15, no. 1 (Special Issue on Multiculturalism). Milwaukee, WI: Rethinking Schools.

This special report of the *Rethinking Schools* journal has a number of important articles that reassess multicultural education, and raise important issues for educators to consider.

Pang, Valerie Ooka. 2001. *Multicultural Education: A Caring-Centered Reflective Approach.* Boston: McGraw-Hill.

Pang delineates six phases to follow in developing caring-centered multicultural education: understand the ethic of caring, review and eliminate prejudice and discrimination, understand the importance of culture, learn and utilize culturally relevant teaching, blend and integrate caring and social justice into teaching and the school, and design and implement classroom and structural school change. Her work is based on theories of Carl Rogers and Jerome Freiberg. The book is brief, with cartoons that help in thinking about negotiating personal and school cultures.

Solorzano, Daniel G., and Tara J. Yosso. 2001. **"From Racial Stereotyping and Deficit Discourse toward a Critical Race Theory in Teacher Education."** *Multicultural Education* 9, no. 1: 2–8.

This article applies critical race theory to teacher education; the five elements of critical race theory provide a framework for teacher education faculty and students to create, re-create, and recover knowledge and art in communities of color.

NONPRINT RESOURCES

Alaska Standards for Culturally Responsive Schools
http://www.ankn.uaf.edu/standards

On-line and pdf format versions of exemplary guidelines for culturally responsive schools. Includes standards for students, educators, curriculum, schools, and communities. Also includes guidelines for preparing culturally responsive teachers, guidelines for culturally responsive libraries, guidelines for respecting cultural knowledge, and an on-line course.

Americanization of the World/Caught between Two Cultures
Videocassette, color, 26 min. (closed captioned). Transcript available in Spanish. Pioneer Living Corp., 2001.

Hosted by Noriyuki "Pat" Morita, this two-part video, targeted to immigrants and multicultural audiences, focuses on positive roles and cross-cultural interaction.

California Department of Education Webpage on Diversity
http://www.cde.ca.gov/iasa/diversity.html

Information and resources in support of diversity as enrichment rather than a source of conflict or divisiveness. Glossary, demographics, English learners, migrant education, interviews with educators, cooperative learning, links to diversity resources.

Critical Pedagogy
http://carbon.cudenver.edu/~mryder/itc_data/crit_ped.html

Sponsored by the University of Colorado at Denver School of Education. Resources, readings, courses.

Disability Direct: Information on Disabilities for Americans
http://www.disability.gov

New Freedom Initiative Web site, sponsored by the U.S. Department of Labor's Office of Disability Employment Policy. Extensive information resources including areas on children and youth, choice and self-determination, civil rights issues, college and adult education, media resources, and disability statistics.

Electronic Magazine of Multicultural Education
http://www.eastern.edu/publications/emme/

On-line magazine for scholars, practitioners, and students of multicultural education.

E-Race It

http://www.crr.ca/eraceit/default.htm

Web site for youth sponsored by the Canadian Race Relations Foundation. History, family, education, employment, media, law, and antiracism.

Global Issues

http://www.globalissues.org/index.html

Extensive links to articles, analysis, and other resources and organizations on "global issues that affect everyone." Includes issues such as poverty, geopolitics (with attention to children), human rights (including racism, women's rights, and justice), environmental issues. Organized by Anup Shah.

In Motion Magazine

http://www.inmotionmagazine.com/

Multicultural on-line U.S. publication about democracy. Includes a forum for voicing opinions and discussion, photographs, and related links.

Institute for People's Education and Action

http://www.peopleseducation.org/

Membership network of the Folk Education Association of America. Supports nonformal education and organizing for social democratic change. Bookshop, member links, summer institute information.

Institute on Community Integration

http://ici.umn.edu/welcome/default.html

Located at the University of Minnesota, this institute works to improve the quality and community orientation of services and supports available to individuals with developmental disabilities and their families. Works with community service providers, school districts, advocacy and self-advocacy organizations, policymakers, and researchers around the world to provide information and practices that support the community integration of individuals with disabilities. Includes information on employment opportunities.

It's Elementary: Talking about Gay Issues in School

http://www.womedia.org/our/elem.html

Video and viewing guide to a highly acclaimed 1997 film by Debra Chasnoff and Helen Cohen. For adult audiences, shot in first- through eighth-grade classrooms across the United States, the film depicts what really happens when educators address gay issues with their students in age-appropriate ways. The film makes a compelling argument that anti-gay prejudice and violence can be prevented if children have an opportunity to have these discussions when they're young. Distributed by New Day Films.

Journal of Critical Pedagogy
http://www.wmc.edu/academics/library/pub/jcp/jcp.html

Biannual refereed electronic publication for interdisciplinary reports of empirical research, theoretical articles, and sociocultural critiques that have implications for critical theory and cultural studies.

Los Angeles County Office of Education
Diverse Student Populations Webpage
http://teams.lacoe.edu/documentation/places/diverse.html

Comprehensive and extensive collection of resources on bilingual education, general diversity and equity, gifted/talented programs, multicultural education, and special needs. Links to other Web sites.

Multicultural Pavilion
http://curry.edschool.virginia.edu/go/multicultural/

Extensive resources and dialogues for educators, students, and activists, sponsored by the University of Virginia's Curry School of Education. Features working definitions and an "assessment toolbox."

National Standards for Parent/Family Involvement Programs
http://www.pta.org/programs/invstand.htm#series

On-line version of the 1997 National PTA's Standards for family involvement. Designed to help leaders in discussion as they develop family involvement programs, as well as for assessment of ongoing reform efforts.

The P.E.R.S.O.N. Project
http://www.youth.org/loco/PERSONProject

Brochure and handbook for lesbian, gay, bisexual, and transgender organizing in kindergarten through twelfth-grade public education in the United States.

Possibilities
http://wwwvms.utexas.edu/~possible/possibil.html

Evolving, on-line dissertation by Anne Shaw and her collaborators at the University of Texas at Austin.

Standards: The International Journal of Multicultural Studies
http://www.colorado.edu/journals/standards/

Electronic journal sponsored by the Office of Diversity and Equity at the University of Colorado, Boulder.

Technology/Pedagogy/Politics: Selected Papers
http://www.mtroyal.ab.ca/critical_visions/papers/papers.htm

Critical visions of new technologies in education, relevant to diversity and multiculturalism.

Utah's Project for Inclusion
http://www.usoe.k12.ut.us/sars/Upi/index.htm

Established in 1990 to promote inclusive education for all students, this site now takes a view of disability as a diversity issue. Assists school districts working proactively on inclusive education in neighborhood schools; serves as a resource for administrators, educators, students, family members, and others; maintains a virtual library on inclusion; and identifies conferences in and out of the state of Utah on inclusive education.

World Racism
http://www.worldracism.com

Current news on race-related issues run by the World News Network. Includes links to sites on the United Nations, immigration, refugees, aid agencies, and crime, as well as links to other race-themed Web sites.

⦾ Glossary

Accountability Language in which much contemporary discussion of education is framed; emphasizes scores on standardized tests and overlooks important issues in multicultural education. Encourages short-term planning that ignores the long-term positive effects of diversity on academic and other achievement.

Additive approach Banks's label for curricula that add culturally relevant material to an already existing curriculum.

Bicultural education Approach to cultural interaction in which students are helped to understand the expectations of more than one culture and to be functional in each. The basis of a mosaic model of multicultural education.

Border literacies Ways of interpreting culture and power in which insider/outsider status is replaced by blurring the boundaries and recognizing multiplicities of identity and group affiliation.

CIVICS Sapon-Shevin's approach to classroom organization and management based on Courage, Inclusion, Value, Integrity, Cooperation, and Safety.

Contributions approach Banks's label for honoring heroes and holidays in school programs.

Creolization The coming together and mixing of diverse cultural traits or elements in order to form new traits or elements.

Critical multicultural education A critical pedagogy approach to multicultural education that signals how questions of audience, voice, power, and evaluation actively work to construct particular relationships between teachers and students, institutions and society, and classrooms and communities.

Critical pedagogy Approach to teaching/learning that takes as a central concern the issue of power in the teaching and learning context, and focuses on how and in whose interests knowledge is produced and transmitted. Pedagogy that illuminates the relationships among knowledge, authority, and power, toward emancipation or liberation.

Cultural democracy approach   Sleeter's label for multicultural education programs that model a pluralist community.

Cultural studies   Cross-disciplinary and anti-disciplinary intellectual movement that stresses the importance of the categories used by and the means of individual subjects to make sense of their worlds and lives; seeks to make relevant former colonial powers' claims to exclusive knowledge production and attends to how various social institutions mediate the production of culture.

Culture-based curricula   Curricula developed through valuing cultures as holistic and culturally specific paradigms, attention to the wisdom of community elders, and participation of all stakeholders in the culture.

Deculturalization   Removal of cultural identity through schooling.

Diversity education   Contemporary variations on multiculturalism and pluralism in education that value multiplicities of identity and recognize complexities, conflict, and collaboration across shifting terrains of group and personal affiliation.

Economies of racism   Structures of economic systems that rely on the perpetuation of racial inequity, with origins in colonial and imperialist practices that today result in abuses of some people in order for others to benefit through international trade.

Encapsulation   An act of closing in, or as if in, a capsule that isolates or separates with a clear boundary.

Essentializing   A process of making things seem fundamentally static and unchangeable by simplifying cultural elements to categories of this seeming reality.

Exceptional and culturally different approach   Sleeter's label for school programs that attempt to accommodate diverse populations within a traditional curriculum.

High-stakes testing   Evaluation programs that demand minimum levels of performance on standardized tests of required curricula.

Human relations approach   Sleeter's label for school programs that facilitate cultural understanding and respect and that foster cross-group collaboration.

Identity   A modernist construct that refers to one's awareness of oneself. In postmodern terms, identity is mulitiple, fluid, and evolving; an ongoing "process of becoming."

Ideology   Ideas, doctrines, or beliefs that form the basis of a political or economic system and inspire individuals, groups, classes, or cultures; sometimes understood as creating ideas for certain inspired groups to use as weapons against other groups.

Immersion bilingual education   Multilingual education in which students alternate the language of instruction and interaction, usually by days or weeks.

Integration   School programs that foster diverse participation across race and ethnicity.

Intercultural education   Old-fashioned precursor to contemporary multicultural education that promoted awareness of other cultures but also entrenched notions of cultural differences as "foreign."

Liberatory pedagogy   Educational practices noted by bell hooks and others that incorporate student perceptions of themselves as critical thinkers participating in a dynamic, fluid environment.

Multicultural education   Precursor to diversity education. Term still currently used in many contexts to represent a range of school programs and policies that respond to diversity and globalization or promote social justice.

Postcolonial   Referring to the historic moments after the period of (European) colonial powers, and the legacy of colonial economic, racial, and geographic dominance of the world by those countries that established colonies.

Racism   The effort, wittingly or through passive neglect, to allocate social status and opportunity to individuals related to their genetic or ethnic background.

Reifying/Reification   The process or act of treating an abstraction or metaphor as if it were something concrete, with size and location, in turn implying a particular "truth" about the world.

Representation   The act or result of making a person, thing, text, action, or image stand for another so that stable and separate identities are reified, implicitly creating the impression that the representation is adequate, accurate, and true.

Segregation   School programs that perpetuate undesired and undemocratic separation of students by race or ethnicity.

Single group studies   Sleeter's label for school programs that study the entire curriculum through a particular social group's history, culture, and perspective on democracy and oppression.

Social action approach   Banks's label for a progressive and highly desirable form of multicultural education in which the curricular experiences and outcomes promote a diverse, pluralist community.

Social justice   The constellation of struggles for race, gender, social class, religious, sexual orientation, and differently abled equality, along with equality based on any other category of difference, together with democratic government, intellectual freedom, environmental protection, and human rights.

Social reconstructionist approach   Sleeter's label for a progressive and highly desirable form of multicultural education in which the curricular experiences and outcomes promote a diverse, just, pluralist community.

Theater of the Oppressed   Method of performance education in which the audience participates in the action; promotes social change through education and public display.

Transformational approach   Banks's label for school programs that are extensively redesigned with multicultural issues and goals in mind.

Whiteness   Cultural term that helps to dismiss the "celebrate diversity" model of multiculturalism in favor of a more complex and useful analysis of race and culture.

White studies   Antiracist and cultural studies that explore whiteness as a legal and political category with aesthetic and cultural value.

☙ Index

About the Author

Peter Appelbaum, associate professor of education at Arcadia University, teaches curriculum theory and math/science/technology education and has been working with urban, suburban and rural schools on multicultural and diversity projects for the last ten years.